Do We Worship
the Same God?

Do We Worship the Same God?

COMPARING
THE
BIBLE
AND
THE
QUR'AN

GEORGE DARDESS

ST. ANTHONY MESSENGER PRESS
Cincinnati, Ohio

RESCRIPT

In accord with the *Code of Canon Law*, I hereby grant my permission to publish *Do We Worship the Same God? Comparing the Bible and the Qur'an* by George Dardess.

Most Reverend Carl K. Moeddel
Vicar General and Auxiliary Bishop
of the Archdiocese of Cincinnati
Cincinnati, Ohio
May 3, 2006

The permission to publish is a declaration that a book or pamphlet is considered to be free from doctrinal or moral error. It is not implied that those who have granted the permission to publish agree with the contents, opinions or statements expressed.

The Scripture quotations contained herein are from the *New Revised Standard Version Bible*, copyright ©1989 by the Division of Christian Education of the National Council of the Churches of Christ in the U.S.A. Used by permission. All rights reserved.

Quotations from the Qur'an are the author's own version.

Cover and book design: Mark Sullivan
Cover photos: istockphoto

LIBRARY OF CONGRESS CATALOGING-IN-PUBLICATION DATA

Dardess, George.
  Do we worship the same God? : comparing the Bible and the Qur'an / George Dardess.
    p. cm.
  Includes index.
  ISBN 0-86716-731-9 (pbk. : alk. paper) 1. Islam—Relations—Christianity. 2. Christianity and other religions—Islam. 3. Koran—Relation to the Bible. 4. Bible—Comparative studies. 5. Koran—Comparative studies. I. Title.

BP172.D3723 2006
261.2'7—dc22

2006009008

ISBN-10: 0-86716-731-9
ISBN-13: 978-0-86716-731-3

Published by St. Anthony Messenger Press
28 W. Liberty St.
Cincinnati, OH 45202
www.AmericanCatholic.org

Printed in the United States of America.

Printed on acid-free paper.

06 07 08 09 10 5 4 3 2 1

CONTENTS

ACKNOWLEDGMENTS

My thanks to Sister Connie Derby, R.S.M., a member of the department of Faith Development Ministry for the Diocese of Rochester, New York, for her invaluable advice in shaping this book based on her experience as a director of religious education.

And very special thanks to Dr. Muhammad Shafiq, Imam of the Islamic Center of Rochester, and to Dr. Aly Nahas for reading this manuscript with a critical eye, but most of all for their warm friendship and support over the years.

INTRODUCTION

Do Christians and Muslims worship the same God?

The question seems moot. Didn't the Second Vatican Council answer it once and for all with a resounding "yes"?

For example, *Lumen Gentium* (Dogmatic Constitution on the Church) boldly proclaimed that:

> ...the plan of salvation also includes those who acknowledge the Creator. In the first place among these are the [Muslims], who, professing to hold the faith of Abraham, along with us adore the one and merciful God, who on the last day will judge [humankind]. (16)

The other relevant Vatican II document, *Nostra Aetate* (Declaration on the Relationship of the Church to Non-Christian Religions), while introducing a complicating factor, also answered this question in the affirmative:

> Upon the [Muslims], too, the Church looks with esteem. They adore one God, living and enduring, merciful and all-powerful, Maker of heaven and earth and Speaker to [humanity]. They strive to submit wholeheartedly even to His inscrutable decrees, just as did Abraham, with whom the Islamic faith is pleased to associate itself. Though they do not acknowledge Jesus as God,

they revere Him as prophet. They also honor Mary, His virgin mother; at times they call on her, too, with devotion. In addition they await the day of judgment when God will give each [person] his due after raising him up. Consequently, they prize the moral life, and give worship to God especially through prayer, almsgiving, and fasting. (3)

Nostra Aetate directly stated what *Lumen Gentium* did not: that Muslims do not worship Jesus as God. Yet in the centuries before Vatican II, that admission had been enough to cause the church to declare a resounding "no!" to this question, and to cause it to condemn Muslims as schismatics. (That's why Dante in *The Divine Comedy* puts Muhammad to gruesome torment in one of the lowest circles of hell.) Vatican II reversed that negative perspective completely. *Nostra Aetate* put the Muslim and Catholic difference of belief about Jesus into a subordinate clause ("Although not acknowledging him as God...") as if the difference of belief, while still very significant, did not outweigh what Muslims and Christians have in common. According to *Nostra Aetate*, the fact that Christians believe that Jesus is God while Muslims don't did not affect the Council's judgment that we do in fact worship the same God.

The Council had good reasons for subordinating the issue of Jesus' divinity in coming to its optimistic conclusion. Much brilliant theological work preparing the way for Muslim-Christian dialogue had already been done in the years leading up to the Council by Louis Massignon (a French scholar of Islam in the twentieth century and priest of the Greek Melkite Rite) and others. We can applaud the Council's effort to overcome centuries of violence and scapegoating in the church's relations with Muslims. But we can still feel uneasy that such a radical reversal of judgment received relatively little elaboration in the Council documents themselves. Lacking that elaboration, the new resounding "yes!" seemed to lack secure grounding and increasingly took on the air of a decision reached from hopefulness alone or from a too-eager desire to make amends. The new resounding "yes!" increasingly seemed fragile, easily vulnerable to changes of mood, both in the Catholic church and outside it.

Those changes were brewing well before the terrorist attacks of September 11, 2001. These attacks erupted in the mass media, issuing in the insistence that a resounding "no!" be given to the question, "Do we worship the same God?" Certain media pundits and even some Christian pastors drew a line of absolute separation between the Christian God and Muslim God, calling the one a God of peace and love, and the other a God, or god, of war and violence. Little evidence for this resounding "no!" was given. Little was apparently needed: Osama Bin Laden's justifications for attacking the World Trade Center towers and the Pentagon were sufficient. The God or god to whom Osama appealed for approval could not in any shape or form be the God worshiped by us, Osama's targets.

Not all questionings of the resounding "yes!" were as divisive as these. In fact, a lot of the questioning that has been emerging since September 11 has been healthy. The question I am asking in this book—Do we worship the same God?—is already being addressed in scholarly journals, not only by Christians and Muslims, but by Jews as well. No simple, single answer has emerged. Yet the interplay of responses has been thoughtful and generous, indicating that, at least for right now, the discussion itself is more important than the answer. What the Second Vatican Council's resounding "yes!" lacked—a grounding in widespread dialogue among Muslims and Christians—is finally being initiated.

This book attempts to bring into that dialogue not experts, but ordinary Catholics (and other open-minded Christians). It does so by providing such readers with a tool they may have so far lacked: informed knowledge of the Muslim scripture, the Qur'an. *Do We Worship the Same God?* asserts that Christians can't talk reasonably about whether we worship the same God as Muslims do unless we first know clearly and accurately what the Qur'an says about God and God's deeds among us and for us. Gaining such knowledge is the indispensable first step. The second step would involve engaging in discussion about God with Muslims themselves. It is one thing to ask, "Do we worship the same God?" among ourselves, as I'm proposing that we do here, using the present book as a guide. It is another to take the bolder step of asking the same question among Muslims. My hope is that the knowledge of Islam gained by using this book will encourage readers to take that next necessary step, confident in their ability to enter into meaningful dialogue with Muslims on a question that concerns us all.

And it is a question that concerns all Christians more deeply after September 11 than before it. September 11 in itself was a disaster, and other disasters—in the form of the loss of thousands of innocent lives in Afghanistan and Iraq—have followed from it. But September 11 has had at least one positive effect. It has made Christians' questions about Islam more serious. Prior to September 11, the question, "Do we worship the same God?" probably seemed for most Christians the sort of thing that only theologians were equipped to talk about. Now, however, "Do we worship the same God?" has become a question of vital interest to all. Whether or not we Christians find ourselves locked, as some would say, in a "civilizational struggle" with Islam, we still need to know what motivates Muslims living around the world and among us. Is their God one of violence? If the answer is "yes," we are all of us, Christians and Muslims alike, in for a lot of trouble. Or is it possible that their God is also not only a God of peace, but the same God we Christians worship, despite our differences about Jesus? If the answer is "yes," we have the strongest possible warrant for working together against terrorism and for peace and justice.

Even if we Christians can't come to a clear answer either way on the question of whether we worship the same God, we will not have wasted our time in our search. Far from it! If our searching for that answer has brought us into meaningful dialogue with our Muslim neighbors, we will have reached a perhaps more important goal than that of being able to answer this question firmly. Our searching will have established human relationships between our two communities of faith. We will have gotten to know each other's names. We will have learned about each other's families, about each other's aches and pains, about each other's fears and hopes. We will have had meals together. Perhaps we will have come up with projects serving not only each other's needs but also those of the larger community. Friendly human ties have a way of opening minds to fresher perspectives. Questions about God, previously confusing or even threatening when approached on a strictly intellectual level, will begin to look intriguing or even fascinating on the level of concrete human exchange. A simple "yes" or "no" answer to, "Do we worship the same God?" might still seem a long way off, but the likelihood of an eventual "yes" will have greatly increased.

And if we are able to arrive at a "yes" in answer to the question, "Do we worship the same God?" then a further opportunity is opened up: the opportunity—the blessing, really—of praying together. Pope John Paul II took this prophetic step at Assisi in 1986 when he prayed for world peace along with the religious leaders of many faiths, including religious leaders of

Islam. Praying with Muslims should be distinguished from worshiping with them, however. Worship is prayer, yes, but it is prayer in public witness to a religion's particular beliefs and traditions. Catholics cannot give such witness no matter how warm their sympathy with Islam. But if we Catholics, following the lead of Vatican II, come to the understanding that we do indeed worship—each in our own distinct way—the same God, we can find ways of praying to that God together without violating our significant differences. We can worship the same God without worshiping him in exactly the same way.

In presenting Islam to Catholics—and other interested Christians—through a comparative study of our holy Scriptures, I decided against a lecturing approach. I wanted to construct the book in such a way that readers could reach their own conclusions about what the Qur'an has to say about God. I didn't want readers to depend on an authoritative voice telling them what to think. The distinction is a tricky one, I admit. A book such as this one cannot avoid speaking authoritatively on many points. Our Western education has provided many of us with next to no knowledge of the Qur'an and almost nothing as well of Islam's history and culture. So orienting readers and giving them basic facts about the Qur'anic texts chosen for discussion are necessary first steps. And they are challenging steps, too, because the Qur'an's treatment of its subject matter is allusive, rather than narrative or expository. Filling in the Qur'an's silences just far enough but not too far has been my goal. I have tried to give readers sufficient means to grapple with the questions on their own. And then I've tried to get out of their way.

The best way to elicit independent thinking—a lesson I learned in my former career as a teacher of English literature—is to present material comparatively. That's the method followed here. Beginning with chapter three, I offer consecutive passages addressing a common topic, one passage (or occasionally two or three) from the Bible and the other passage (or occasionally two or three) from the Qur'an. The reader will need help in approaching these texts, particularly the Qur'anic one. That's why the passages selected for each chapter are preceded by a brief introduction outlining the particular issue addressed. Then following the consecutive passages comes the heart of each chapter: several guided reflection questions. The questions themselves often contain additional information to help the reader see exactly what is at issue in a particular Qur'anic wording or silence. Framing this overall pattern are chapters one and two, which give background on Islam and on the Qur'an, and the conclusion, where the lines of questioning developed in the book will be summarized. Throughout the book the purpose is to educate readers on both their own scriptures and on the Qur'an, not judging the texts or rating their theological validity, but enabling readers to decide for themselves from textual evidence how the God we Catholics and Muslims worship might be the same or different—or perhaps both at the same time!

Do We Worship the Same God? is designed for use either by a parish adult study group or by individuals at their own pace. For group meetings I recommend, after prayer (such as the prayer included after this Introduction) and a review of the chapter's introductory information, that both the biblical and Qur'anic texts be read aloud slowly and meditatively. Then the group is ready to engage in the reflection questions. My hope, as I said earlier, is that the sessions would eventually stimulate the group to want to invite a local Muslim group to engage in joint discussion of these or other comparative texts. I have facilitated such a discussion in my hometown, with delightfully enlightening results for participants of both faiths.

Finally, three points of information that may be useful to the reader.

The first is about the biblical and Qur'anic texts used. All biblical quotations included are from the *New Revised Standard Version* of the Bible. The translations of the Qur'an (or "versions," as Muslims prefer to say—for reasons given in chapter two) are my own. Each verse number has been included for easy reference.

The second point concerns the way chapters (or *suras*) and verses of the Qur'an are referred to. *Sura* 4:123, for example, means *sura* (or chapter) 4, verse 123. Unlike the Bible, the Qur'an is not a compilation of separate writings by different authors or editors. It is a compilation of oral revelations that came down to one man, Muhammad, over a twenty-two-year period. That is why it is composed of chapters rather than individual books, letters, gospels or the like.

The third point concerns the use of the pronoun "he" when referring to God. Both Christianity and Islam agree that God is beyond all gender—in fact, Islam is more insistent upon this point than Christianity is, since Islam strictly forbids all imaging of God that would seem to make God look human in any way. So, for instance, no picture of God or even of Muhammad can be found in any mosque. Yet because the word for God in Arabic—Allah—has the masculine grammatical gender and because all English versions of the Qur'an known to me use "he" as the pronoun referring to Allah, I have decided to use "he" in referring to God in my translation of Qur'anic texts—and in biblical ones too.

Although in the course of the centuries many quarrels and hostilities have arisen between Christians and [Muslims], this most sacred Synod urges all to forget the past and to strive sincerely for mutual understanding. On behalf of all [humankind], let them make common cause of safeguarding and fostering social justice, moral values, peace, and freedom.

—*Nostra Aetate*, 3

OPENING PRAYER

(This prayer may be used by groups or individuals at the beginning of each chapter.)

God, creator of us all, master of the universe,
we ask you to be present with us
as we search to know you
not only in our own sacred scripture
but also in that of our Muslim sisters and brothers.
Help us forget past quarrels
as well as present fears and suspicions.
Help us instead to keep our minds open,
our spirits free,
and our hearts joyful
as we ponder:
whether the God we both worship
is you.
Amen.

PART ONE

BACKGROUND AND ORIENTATION

CHAPTER ONE

ISLAM AND THE LIFE OF MUHAMMAD

The Change

Answering questions about Islam used to be easy. People used to come to my talks on Islam with an attitude of polite curiosity. Not knowing much or anything about this unfamiliar religion practiced by people living on the other side of the Earth, they hoped to be informed. To those audiences Islam was an interesting, exotic topic, something for the specialist, to be sure, but still something important enough to know a little bit about.

September 11, 2001, changed all that, and much besides. To some extent, this was a change for the good. Many people's previous attitudes had been somewhat complacent, their broad-mindedness untested. Now their questions about Islam couldn't be asked from a comfortable distance. Who were these people who crashed the airplanes into the World Trade Center towers and the Pentagon? What did it mean that they were Muslims and that they claimed to be carrying out the Holy War or Jihad supposedly prescribed for them in their holy book, the Qur'an? What did it mean that they expected to go straight to the bliss of heaven as their reward? How could a religion that motivated such violence *not* be a violent one? How could such a religion not be seen as a threat—a threat not only to American lives and world peace, but even to Christianity itself?

But if this change in attitudes toward Islam post–September 11 has had its upside, it has had its disadvantages as well. The tone in which some people now tend to ask questions about Islam—anxious, even fearful—means that it is very difficult to talk calmly about facts. But facts are where we have to begin, especially with the facts of Islam's early history.

The Rise of Islam

Islam is the name we give to the religion of about 1.3 billion people—roughly as many as the number of Roman Catholic Christians worldwide. And just as Christianity began with a small group of disciples gathering around a charismatic founder, so too did Islam. Both religions have their roots in local reforms of established practices. Both contained within them a dynamism which quickly transformed a local reform into a universal one that embraced all humankind.

For Christianity, this transformation was brought about by the death and resurrection of Jesus Christ. For Islam, it was brought about by the prophet Muhammad's *hijrah,* or migration from Mecca to Medina with a small band of his persecuted followers. These climactic changes had their origins in previous divine interventions. For Christians, the incarnation of God in Jesus Christ marks that initial intervention. For Muslims, the divine intervention is the outpouring of verbal revelations sent down by Allah (not a special name peculiar to Islam but simply the Arabic word for God) to the prophet Muhammad over a twenty-two-year period, from AD 610 to Muhammad's death in AD 632. The revelations were collected soon after Muhammad's death in the book known as the Qur'an, or "Reciting."

Muhammad in Mecca, AD 570–610

Muhammad was born in AD 570 in Mecca, an ancient town located at an oasis near the north-south trade route running along the western side of the Arabian Peninsula. Although he came from the dominant Quraysh tribe ruling Mecca at the time, Muhammad grew up with two disadvantages. One was that he was born into a relatively weak clan within the Quraysh tribe. The other and more serious disadvantage was that he was orphaned as a child. Muhammad's father died before he was born, his mother when he was six, his grandfather when he was eight. Luckily for him, Muhammad then found shelter with his uncle. Being an orphan would not have been such a problem in the Bedouin society of Mecca's past where harsh desert conditions and a nomadic lifestyle tended to enforce the value of every male tribal member. However, that nomadic lifestyle was gradually changing. Camel trade through Mecca had been increasing in recent decades, and so a more settled, entrepreneurial, individualistic social system had begun to emerge. Wealth in Mecca was concentrated in fewer and fewer hands, instead of being spread out more or less evenly as in the old tribal days. Concern for the common good began to weaken. As a result, each of the deaths in Muhammad's family—of mother, father and grandfather—left him helpless and undefended. Muhammad had firsthand experience of this change of mores. Much of the ethical passion of the Qur'an reflects Muhammad's own outrage at the Quraysh's lack of care for the weak and vulnerable.

The Quraysh were growing rich from another source as well: from the annual *hajj*, or pilgrimage, traffic of the various outlying tribes to Mecca to visit the Ka'bah, the ancient cube-like structure thought to mark the place of creation. The Ka'bah was used then as a depository for each tribe's god. Some 360 idols were said to be located in or near this cultic center. The Quraysh charged fees for the yearly visits of the tribes to the Ka'bah during a month of peace from more or less constant inter-tribal warfare.

During his early years in Mecca, Muhammad, distinguished by his truthfulness, was given the nickname of *el-amin*, the reliable one. It was apparently for this quality that he was hired at age twenty-five by a woman fifteen years older than he named Khadijah to lead her camel caravans to Syria in the north and to carry out trade there. He returned with a profit. Impressed by his commercial skills and probity and struck by him personally, she proposed marriage, which he accepted. They lived together monogamously and by all accounts happily until her death in AD 621. Their life together changed dramatically in AD 610 when Muhammad received the first of the revelations that became the Qur'an. Muhammad was shaken by this event. Were the revelations truly from God? Or had they been inspired by a jinn (a creature made of flame—from which we derive the word "genie")? Khadijah strengthened her husband's confidence not only in the authenticity of the revelations but in his role as prophet.

The Message and Meaning of Islam
That task was to do what all prophets previous to him had done, to remind humankind of its commitment to the one God and to the one God alone. The reminder had to take the form of a warning, because humankind had drifted far from its commitment. It is in this sense that we spoke earlier of Islam, as well as of Christianity, as religious reform movements. If Christianity began as a reform movement within Judaism, Islam began as a reform movement within the polytheistic culture of Muhammad's hometown of Mecca.

At a later point, Islam sought to reform what it saw as serious errors in both Judaism and Christianity. But the main thrust of the entire Qur'an and of the vast body of Muslim theology, law and spirituality that grew from it is directed against idolatry: against what the Qur'an calls *shirk,* or the association of any other deity, ideology or public or private obsession with God. "There is no god but God" forms the first part of the *shahadah,* or confession, the first of the Five Pillars of Islam (along with *salat,* or daily public prayer; *zakat,* or almsgiving; *sawm,* or fasting, especially during the sacred month of Ramadan; and *hajj,* or pilgrimage to Mecca). "There is no god but God" means that the gods of Mecca and everywhere else where people's ultimate allegiance is given to an idol are as nothing. Islam's vigorous assertion of monotheism, along with its equally vigorous assertion that Muhammad is the messenger of this truth, is the heart and soul of its creed.

The creed demands human response, and Islam is its name. While the word *Islam* has been used for the past two centuries as a name distinguishing the religion of Muslims from other religions, the word's root meaning refers to the act of handing oneself over as a hostage in a treaty arrangement. A common translation of the word Islam is "submission." But the word "submission" suggests forced obedience, a tactic diametrically opposed to the Qur'an's injunction, "Let there be no compulsion in religion" (*sura* 2:256). The word Islam more accurately means "self-yielding" and as such captures exactly what we Christians pray when we say, "Thy will be done." Other forms of the word Islam are the word *muslim,* referring to the person who yields him or herself totally to God; and the word *salaam,* which, like the Hebrew *shalom,* refers to peace with all creation through fullness of life and relationships.

Despite the caricatures of Islam one sometimes hears in the media and even from some Christian pastors, the God to whom

Muslims yield themselves is not a God of wrath. Just as Catholic Christians say "in the name of the Father, Son and Holy Spirit" in order to acknowledge, humbly, our place within the Trinitarian relationship, Muslims say "in the name of God, the most beneficent and merciful" to acknowledge their relation to the God who seeks their flourishing. It is important to recognize, however, that the relationships Muslims and Christians acknowledge by these formulas, even if made with the same God, are nevertheless fundamentally different. One of the key goals of this book is to enable those who use it to clarify what this difference is. What needs to be emphasized right now is that the God evoked by Muslims is a God marked by overflowing generosity. "Most beneficent" refers to God's free gift of creation itself. "Most merciful" refers to God's tireless willingness to forgive us our failings. Both words in Arabic are intensive forms. "Most beneficent" really means that God is beyond all measurement of beneficence. "Most merciful" means that he is beyond all measurement of mercy. The point is that the Muslim approaches God, not in abject fear, but in the profoundest gratitude.

This gratitude is expressed not only in worship but also in service to others. Central to Islam is its ethical dimension. The God to whom Muslims yield themselves is the God of creation. Since God desires that creation flourish, humankind is obliged to serve that desire by acting as God's *khalifah,* or vice-regents. The obligation entails on humankind a concern for the poor and marginalized and for the equitable use of material resources. In a sense, Islam returns humankind to the practice of the nomadic Bedouins by instilling once again in believers a lively concern for the common good. But while in the old polytheistic days this concern grew mostly out of a practical need to conserve scant resources, including human ones, the concern is now rooted in obedience to the God of creation and in fear of the Day of Judgment, a belief foreign to the this-worldly Bedouins but central, as the Qur'an insisted, to the prophesies brought to the various tribes of humankind over the ages, beginning with Abraham, continuing through Moses and Jesus, and concluding with Muhammad. In this new—or, rather, restored—ethical dimension, the arrogance, the glorying in violence, and the pursuit of revenge—all key elements of male Bedouin behavior—were overthrown in favor of humility, moderation and social stability. Overthrown too were practices that devalued or victimized women. Islam outlawed the killing of unwanted female babies, as well as the treatment of women as chattel in marriage arrangements.

Muhammad in Mecca, AD 610–622

At first the Quraysh were not bothered by Muhammad's preaching. The word "Allah" was familiar to them as the name of the transcendent deity. They honored this deity, but preferred to worship their tribal idols since the idols seemed easier to approach. Muhammad appeared to be doing little more than adding a different emphasis to the already pluralistic religious environment which had become the Quraysh's bread and butter.

But as the number of disciples around Muhammad grew, the Quraysh became aware that the Allah who spoke through Muhammad was no Zeus, content to tolerate other gods as long as they played second fiddle. Allah insisted, as I noted earlier, that the other gods were nothing. This radical claim undermined the very basis for the hajj trade. How could that trade continue if the very purpose of the hajj—to honor the 360 tribal idols—was declared an utter lie and offense to the one and only God?

The Quraysh were also alarmed by the high ethical demands being imposed on them by God. It was bad enough that their pocketbooks were being threatened. Perhaps just as bad or even worse was that their arrogance and individualism were being called into question. The Quraysh reacted predictably. They began to persecute the followers of the new religion. Since most (but not all) of Muhammad's first disciples came from disadvantaged social groups—youths, impoverished clan members and women—the persecution had an effect, so much so that Muhammad recommended that the most vulnerable of them seek asylum with the Christian King of Abyssinia.

Thanks to his uncle, Muhammad himself felt relatively safe from the Quraysh's persecution. Then, in AD 621, a crisis occurred. In this year his two strongest supports, his wife, Khadijah, and his uncle, both died. Muhammad was again left defenseless. What was he to do? His life was threatened. But even worse: It looked as if the bold announcements of God's oneness and of humankind's moral responsibility to each other's well-being—the announcements God had asked him to make not only to the Quraysh but to all humankind—would come to nothing. Muhammad's failure seemed to portend the failure of God himself to make God's voice heard.

Muhammad seemed to have reached a dead end. His ministry in his hometown of Mecca, like Jesus' ministry in Galilee, had had initial success, but then had come up against great obstacles. He had to make a bold move if his movement was to flourish.

The Hijrah, AD 622
The move Muhammad then made was as critical for his own future and for the future of the movement he had founded as was Jesus' decision to go to Jerusalem.

Muhammad decided to transplant himself and his entire band of followers—probably fewer than a hundred people—to an agricultural town two or three hundred miles to the north called Yathrib. He sent his followers out in small groups so as not to call the Quraysh's attention to what was afoot. Then Muhammad stole away from town in the night accompanied by his friend Abu Bakr. The Quraysh got wind of Muhammad's escape and almost caught and killed him. But Muhammad made it safely to Yathrib, thereafter called *Medinat-al-nabi* ("City of the Prophet") or simply Medina. It was here in Medina that Islam as it is today known came into its own. The decisive journey from Mecca to Medina is known as the *hijrah* or emigration.

What made Yathrib attractive to Muhammad was that members of two powerful tribes of that town had already invited him there to help them settle disputes that were threatening to turn into out-and-out warfare. Muhammad accepted the invitation on condition that the tribes in question accept Islam. When the tribes agreed to the conditions, Muhammad's escape route from danger in Mecca was clear. And in short order he brought peace to the tribes that had invited him. Yet Muhammad never saw his separation from Mecca as permanent. He knew that Islam would never become the religion of the Arabs unless Mecca became its base. So he undertook the *hijrah* as a step that would ultimately assure the conversion of the Quraysh and the cleansing of the Ka'bah. A mere eight years later these very events came to pass.

The years between were spent in consolidating Islam's community life. The community changed from a persecuted remnant to a kind of super-tribe based on egalitarian principles. As the community changed, so did Muhammad. From a vulnerable prophetic voice on the fringe, Muhammad became lawgiver and judge to the new community. He also became the general in charge of its defense when he found it necessary to protect the community against the efforts of the Quraysh and other rival tribes to destroy it. This is the part of Islam's history that has been grievously distorted both by Islam's enemies and by

Islam's own extremists. The wars Muhammad undertook during this period were defensive wars. *Jihad* (from the Arabic for "striving for a good end") was evoked to rally the community to war against particular enemies. But the conditions under which war was to be engaged were rigorously restricted. These restrictions closely resemble those that emerge in Christianity's own doctrine of the "Just War." For example, both Jihad and Just War theory forbid injury to noncombatants. In no case did Muhammad or the Qur'an speak of wholesale slaughter or "holy war." (See chapter fifteen for a fuller treatment of this distinction.)

Another part of Islam's history that has been distorted is Muhammad's taking of several wives during the Medina period. Even though polygamy was regularly practiced in seventh-century Arabia, Muhammad's marriages were necessary to seal the fidelity of disparate clans and families to the new community. Many of the revelations that came to Muhammad during the Medina period have in fact to do with the establishment and safeguarding of women's rights, a concept unknown in Bedouin culture.

Muhammad Returns to Mecca, AD 630
In AD 630, after three major battles with the Quraysh, Muhammad entered in triumph the city from which he had emigrated eight years before. Contrary to expectation, he did not put Mecca's male inhabitants—previously his fiercest enemies—to the sword or enslave its women and children. He did not even force conversion to Islam. His entry was a peaceful one, intended to break the deadly cycle of vengeful reprisals that had previously characterized Bedouin tribal conflicts. He restored the Ka'bah to its primordial condition as the site of the altar Adam himself had built to the glory of the one God—the altar that Abraham and his son Ishmael had rebuilt and that now once again became the

center of prophetic monotheism for all humankind. With the cultic center now cleansed, Muhammad turned outward, encouraging the new *ummah* (community) to expand toward the boundaries of Arabia and beyond. While Muhammad himself died only two years later, the energy generated by his return to Mecca caused Islam to spread within a hundred years from Spain to the West to the Oxus River in the East.

Yet the two religious groups—the Jews and Christians—that had carried the prophetic tradition forward up to Muhammad's time were not invited to the restored cultic center in Mecca or to participate in the expansion. Both groups, says the Qur'an, had long ago heard exactly the same message Muhammad had heard: the message that humankind was to serve God and God alone and to care for each other as equally loved creations of this one God. Muhammad never claimed to be bringing a new religion to humankind but to be reforming the ancient and only true one. Yet Jews and Christians—whom Muhammad had originally expected would welcome this latest sign of God's concern—not only kept their distance from the new *ummah* of Muhammad, but also, at least in the case of certain (not all) of the Jewish tribes of Medina, they proved to be actively and even treacherously hostile to it. Of the two groups, the Qur'an considers Christians closest in spirit and practice to the reform brought through Muhammad. And yet we Christians had gone dangerously astray, says the Qur'an, by practicing *shirk*—that is, by turning the honored prophet Jesus into a divinity and associating him as if on an equal basis with the one God. Still, despite the disappointed hope of achieving unity among Jews, Christians and Muslims, the Qur'an never rejects Jews or Christians altogether from their honored positions as "People of the Book." Nor does the Qur'an endorse the *ummah* of Muhammad as a perfected community. The Qur'an warns all of humankind, Muslims as severely as Christians and Jews, that human weakness, manifested in hypocrisy, injustice and violence, remains a persistent and universal threat. No human group, Muslim or any other, can rely on its own strength or religious pedigree to cope with that threat successfully. Only true self-yielding to God's mercy or grace can save us.

Muhammad and Jesus

We will consider Jesus' role in Islam more closely in subsequent chapters. But to end the present chapter, we can establish a parallel between Muhammad's and Jesus' careers as prophets. Of course, we Christians regard Jesus as far more than a prophet. The parallel can go only so far. Yet even that distance is enough to give us a clearer picture of what it is that makes our respective faiths both so similar and so different.

Let's return to the climactic decisions Muhammad and Jesus made, decisions that established the success of their respective missions. Muhammad's decision, to leave Mecca behind him and undertake a *hijrah* to Yathrib, made possible his later triumphant entry into Mecca. Once firmly established in Mecca, Islam developed a powerful centrifugal thrust that carried it outward within a century across vast expanses of the known world. Jesus' corresponding decision also led to a triumph, one that would empower his followers to "make disciples of all nations" (see Matthew 28:19). Yet by leaving behind the relative safety of Galilee and going up to Jerusalem for the Passover, Jesus moved toward the cultic center, in this case Jerusalem, not away from it. And where Muhammad sought to escape persecution in order to build up his community, Jesus built up his community by the opposite tactic: by entering right into the teeth of the persecution and death he knew awaited him in Jerusalem. Yes, Jesus entered the cultic center triumphantly on Palm Sunday. But where Muhammad's triumphal entry into Mecca in AD 630 was the direct prelude both to his success as prophet and to the *ummah*'s worldwide expansion, Jesus' triumphal entry led shortly afterward to his scapegoating and victimization and to the scattering of his followers.

From the point of view of Muslims, the parallelism cannot be carried further, because Muslims cannot accept Jesus' death and resurrection: the events that for Christians subsequently transform what otherwise must seem either a foolhardy or suicidal decision on Jesus' part into the key step that led to Christianity's ultimate flourishing and expansion throughout the world. What the Qur'an says about Jesus' death and resurrection will be treated in a later chapter. For now it is enough to see that Muhammad's decision to emigrate from Mecca follows naturally from the central fact that all Muslims assert about him: that he was a human being. As a human being, he made a rational decision in AD 622–a decision based on knowledge of his own human limitations and on an appraisal of what safeguarding his movement would entail. Muslims will not make a greater claim about Muhammad because to do so would be to commit the worst of all sins in Islam, the sin of *shirk* or idolatry. The fact that we Christians do not feel such restraint, the fact that we even make that greater claim "boastfully" (in Saint Paul's words), not about Muhammad, of course, but about a fellow prophet, Jesus, is either a permanent stumbling block in our relationship with Muslims or an opportunity for the most searching dialogue with them, one that promises to enhance both our faiths.

It is easy to see how the Christian claim that Jesus is divine (or, conversely, the Muslim claim that Jesus was only human) could be a stumbling block. It is less easy to see how the possibility of mutual enrichment could flow from directly engaging such a difference of view. Yet it is the purpose of the present book to open up the possibility of such enrichment, even at the point when dialogue seems impossible.

CHAPTER TWO

THE QUR'AN AS SIGN OF GOD

A Book in the Tabernacle

To get an idea of the status of the Qur'an among Muslims, imagine opening the tabernacle door in your church and finding the Bible inside instead of the ciborium with the consecrated hosts.

How would you react to this replacement? Of course you would feel at a loss. The sacrament of God's presence in the eucharistic bread and wine had disappeared! But how would you feel about what had replaced it, the Bible? Would you believe that God, absent in one form, could be fully present in another, in his Word? Would your belief in God's presence in the Word be strong enough to compensate for the loss of God's presence in the bread and wine?

Such questions aren't meant seriously, of course. Thanks to Vatican II, we see the proclamation of the Word and the consecration of the bread and wine as equally integral parts of the eucharistic action. They cannot be separated. The sacrament cannot be limited to either one. And Eucharist requires other key elements as well—the gathering of the people and the presiding of the priest—for its full realization.

Yet, as *Sacrosanctum Concilium* (Constitution on the Sacred Liturgy) says, "[Christ] is present...especially under the Eucharistic species" (7). We Catholics do privilege the consecrated bread and wine as especially effective signs of the exchange of gifts between God and humankind—especially effective because Christ is present there personally and substantially. As for God's Word, its sacramental nature is realized in its proclamation within the liturgy. We do not point to the physical book, the Bible itself, as a sacramental sign.

Muslims do not point in that way to the Bible either, but for a different reason.

As mentioned in the previous chapter, the Qur'an considers both Jews' and Christians' worship of God to have been corrupted. The Jews' worship of God was corrupted by their self-confessed infidelity to God and by their exclusiveness (calling themselves God's "chosen people"). Christians corrupted their prophet's (Jesus') teaching by turning the prophet himself into a god.

But because the Qur'an regards itself as the purest, most direct form of God's message to humankind, Muslims treat it as the physical sign of God's presence among us: the sign of God's presence, not in body and blood, but in word proclaimed and written. In the Qur'an God speaks directly to humankind. There is no intermediary voice in the Qur'an: no narrator, no human speaker at all—not even the voice of Muhammad. For Muslims, God and God alone is heard, in tones as fresh and vibrant as those in which God first delivered them to Muhammad fourteen hundred years ago. For Muslims, the Qur'an contains God's voice speaking to humankind now, in its present condition, just as it will speak to the last person left alive to hear it. For Muslims, to respond to that voice is to enter into a relationship with God that enables human fruition both in this world and in the next.

The effect is not unlike what happens to us Catholics when we receive Eucharist.

"Not unlike"—there's the rub. Sacred as the Qur'an and the consecrated blood and wine are as signs, they are not equivalent. Both regarded by their respective communities as precious gifts of God to humankind, they are nevertheless gifts of different kinds. For this reason, the Qur'an cannot be called a sacrament, since the word sacrament distinguishes the particular gift that is the body and blood of Christ. And as Catholics, we are not in a position to assert that the Qur'an (or any other non-Christian holy text or practice) directly mediates God's grace. Neither the documents of Vatican II nor subsequent papal pronouncements anywhere make such an assertion. Yet they do not categorically and unambiguously deny the possibility.

Caution is in order here. We Christians cannot, in our enthusiasm for dialogue, blur the distinction between sign and sacrament. Muslims would not tolerate such blurring any more than we would. Muslims would never say that God's presence is mediated to them in the Qur'an in the same or similar way as Christ's presence is mediated to us under the appearance of bread and wine in the act of liturgical worship. Yet Christians and Muslims both assert that mediation through Eucharist and Qur'an does certainly occur.

For the sake of dialogue, Christians and Muslims need to honor the difference between our respective understandings of how God has revealed and continues to reveal himself to our communities. But in order to respect a difference, we need to understand as clearly as we can what the difference is. Understanding begins with Muslims' and Catholics' restraining our tendency to want to judge between sign and sacrament. Honest dialogue depends upon having enough confidence in our own religious identity to be able to explore the religious identity of others without tension or defensiveness. It is the sort of confidence that those truly strengthened by the sacrament and sign of their respective religions—whether by the Eucharist or the Qur'an—are most likely to exhibit. Those who love the Eucharist will be able to imagine the love Muslims have for the Qur'an, based on the principle that only lovers understand other lovers.

The Challenge
The greatest challenge to Christians' understanding of the Qur'an might not be doctrinal. It just might be linguistic. This is because the voice in which God speaks to humankind in the Qur'an is Arabic. And since Muslims treasure this voice above all things, the Qur'an's appeal will remain difficult to appreciate without some understanding of the Arabic language.

Bad news indeed! Understanding a bare minimum of Arabic is not like understanding a bare minimum of French or Spanish. French and Spanish might have given us fits in high school, but at least we can recognize some of the vocabulary and maybe even understand a little bit if people speak very slowly and clearly.

None of that is going to happen with Arabic.

For one thing, the Arabic alphabet looks totally different from our Roman one. It has more letters (twenty-nine) as well. Some of our key word sounds are not even represented (there is no *p* or *v*, for example), while some other sounds are represented that we don't form at all in English, unless we're clearing our throat or choking. And to top it all off, Arabic is written backward, from right to left.

But even if we manage to learn the alphabet, we reach another roadblock. The language itself is not an Indo-European language. It is a Semitic one, like Hebrew. It is based on different principles of word formation from Indo-European languages. The roots of the words are different too. We wouldn't recognize the great majority of them even if they were written out in our own alphabet. And the few words we do recognize—words like Jihad, Allah, Muslim and Islam itself—have so lost connection with their original context that they've become more truly English words than Arabic ones. The words convey our own understanding of Islam, not the understanding of Muslims themselves. And the gap between those understandings has grown profound.

The fact that languages can express that gap and even help bring it about shouldn't surprise us. Languages are far more than assemblages of alphabets and sounds and dictionaries. They are carriers and indeed progenitors of cultural values. So what makes Arabic truly "difficult" isn't simply its alphabet and the rest. Arabic is "difficult" primarily because the culture the language carries and helps shape is very different from ours.

Consider how much easier French and Spanish are in this respect. French and Spanish belong to and are expressive of a common cultural sphere, that of "our" Western civilization, the civilization produced by the European Enlightenment, the civilization we look on at times as humankind's greatest achievement, the one against which we must measure all other civilizations.

This includes the civilization of Islam. Culturally, we in the West have for centuries been locked in competition with the broader cultural and political reality of Islam. Over the centuries the competition has been violent. Over the centuries our cultures have taken turns holding sway over each other. For the past two hundred years, however, the political and military advantage has been with the West. Yet on September 11 we in the West seemed suddenly to have lost that dominant position when the two prime symbols of our secular culture, the World

Trade Center and the Pentagon, were attacked. Events since that time have seen the West, represented by the governments of the United States and Britain, seeking to regain the advantage. What the outcome of this bloody struggle for hegemony will be only time will tell. In the meantime our own Western perceptions of the Arabic world—and of the Qur'an, which plays such a powerful role in the shaping of that world—will continue to be affected by complex and unpredictable forces of conflict.

As we Christians attempt through this book or through other means to enter into fruitful dialogue with Islam, we need to be aware of the complexity of the cultural, historical and political forces that are shaping both the urgency of such dialogue—as well as the resistance to it on the part of many, including many Christians.

The Qur'an as Work of Beauty
The phrase "work of beauty" must sound strange to those of us who have attempted to read the Qur'an straight through even in an English translation. Certain translations are so stiff and stilted that any honest reader has to come away feeling repulsed. Even the most fluent translations seem somehow pale or distant. Yet even if we manage to look past the quality of the translation, we still seem to find little that is rewarding. For example, we don't find the stories and narratives we find in our own Bible. We find tantalizing allusions to familiar stories (such as the story of the exodus) and to unfamiliar ones. But for the most part the Qur'an seems to be one long moral lecture from beginning to end. So exactly what does it mean to call it a "work of beauty"?

Perhaps my own experience can serve as an illustration of what might be meant. I myself became aware of the Qur'an as a work of beauty by a very gradual process.

Thanks to the generosity of the people of the Islamic Center of Rochester, New York, I, a Roman Catholic Christian, have been able to learn there the basics of Arabic and then afterward to study the Qur'an in Arabic with one of the Center's members. My Qur'an study proceeded in the time-honored way of example and repetition. My teacher would sound out the Qur'anic line according to strict rules of intonation and pacing, and I would try my best to copy him. My teacher would patiently correct my many errors. Then he would help me translate the line literally. We would occasionally discuss the larger significance of the lines we read on a particular day. But my teacher preferred that I grasp the basic meanings first.

At first, progress was very slow. But certain features of the Qur'an's way of speaking came to my aid. One was repetition of key phrases and expressions. I began to notice what these were and to look for them. Two other helpful features were frequent rhyming and word rhythms, especially in the earlier *suras* or chapters. A fourth feature was the extraordinary power of Arabic word formation. Instead of coining new words for new ideas, as English tends to do, Arabic develops new meanings by adding vowels, prefixes and suffixes to basic words. This practice means that each word carries with it in latent form a wide variety of its other meanings. What the Arabic word lacks in precision (since, to the Western learner, there does not appear to be separate words for separate things), it makes up for in poetic compression.

I began to understand now why Muslims said of the language of the Qur'an—indeed, the Qur'an says this about itself—that it possesses *ijaz* or uniqueness and so cannot be imitated or translated. (Muslims refer to the Qur'an in languages other than Arabic as "versions" rather than "translations.") I began also to see my sessions with my teacher in a different light. The teaching method he employed—imitation and repetition—had much in common with musical training, where one sits at the feet of a master absorbing the basic practice into one's body and bones. Reflection and freedom of expression come later, once the foundation has been laid.

I learned about that higher practice by accident. As I walked into the *masjid,* or main prayer area, of the center one afternoon, I heard someone reciting lines I'd already studied. But the manner in which the person recited them was very different from the strict methodical way I'd been learning from my teacher. This reciter's voice followed all the rules my teacher had taught me. But the reciter's voice took advantage of the prescribed pacing in order to soar free in trills and arpeggios that sounded almost operatic. I was amazed by the expressiveness of the recitation. I felt its power touch my heart and instill in me a kind of joyful longing.

I quickly learned that the person reciting those lines was a well-known Qari, or professional Qur'an reciter, who had come from Pakistan to spend some time at the center. I also found out that my impression of the "operatic" quality of his recitation was misleading. Although in Muslim countries Qaris often compete with each other to achieve fame for their Qur'anic recitations, the Qaris are not, like opera stars, trying to call attention to themselves or to the emotion expressed by the operatic character. The best Qaris are trying instead to bring out the inherent beauty of the Qur'an in service to the voice of God speaking through it and through the Qari reciting it. The best Qaris help reveal the Qur'an's nature as sign.

I had heard that in Muslim countries traffic comes to a stop when a radio broadcast of a famous Qari is played over a loudspeaker, and I had wondered how this could happen. Would Christian drivers hurriedly park their cars and listen raptly even to a skilled proclaimer reading the Gospels over a loudspeaker? But now, after hearing the Qari at the Islamic Center, I could sympathize with those drivers. What brought their cars to a halt was the beauty of the voice itself making present the gift of God as it had come down first to Muhammad and as it now resounded for them in the midst of the tumult and confusion of life.

Like all beauty, the voice opened up a vista of *salaam*, peace, true well-being, the fulfillment of all relationships on earth and in heaven.

The Reciting

To say that the Qari or any Muslim "recites the Qur'an" is redundant because the word *qur'an* in Arabic means reciting.

In AD 610 Muhammad withdrew, as was his custom when opportunity arose, to a cave near Mecca to meditate. On one of these occasions, unexpectedly and with a vehemence that made him fearful and doubtful of his own sanity, a revelation came down to him. The revelation took an auditory rather than a visual form. It said: *iqra* or "Recite!"

> Recite! in the name of your Lord, who created
> Created humankind out of a blood clot
> Recite! for your Lord is most generous
> Who taught by the word
> Taught humankind what it did not know....
> (sura al-'alaq "The Clot of Blood" [or "embryo"] 96:1–5)

Nearly a year went by before Muhammad received another revelation, another reciting, another qur'an. But those first five lines give the essence of the rest.

The Qur'an is above all else a revelation to the ear and to the understanding. It is the voice of divine wisdom. But because of our human limitations, we cannot hear that voice directly. So God chose two earthly instruments in which his voice might resonate at a level understandable to us. God's choice purified those instruments, raising them to an extraordinary state of sensitivity. The two earthly instruments transformed in this way were the language of the reciting, Arabic, and the reciter, Muhammad himself.

Yet God did not intend the transformation of a particular human language and of a particular human being as ends in themselves. The Qur'an tends to bypass Muhammad's own personal situation for the sake of the role he must play for others, that of conveying through recitation the message given him. And while the immediate audience for that message would necessarily be his family, followed by his clan, and then all the people of Mecca, the reciting could not be confined there. No local god, no god confined to a particular tribe, had sent this message. The sender was the Lord of all, who "created humankind out of a blood clot"—who took such a humble coagulation of semen and egg and transformed it into beings capable of receiving divine instruction. And in so doing the Lord of all performed an act of unfathomable generosity to which the proper human response is "Islam," which means self-yielding.

The teaching that continues to be conveyed through the various revelations or *wahy* known collectively as the Qur'an is directed to the will. The Qur'an is tireless in its insistence on the ethical transformation of its listeners. While it might seem that such an emphasis is restrictive—as if the only appeal necessary for our well-being is to our human reason alone—the impression is mistaken. The Qur'an appeals to the heart and imagination as well, and very powerfully so. The beauty conveyed through recitation is one manifestation of that appeal. So is the calligraphy with which the Qur'an has traditionally been written down. Muslim architectural and design motifs are derived from calligraphic renderings of the written Qur'an. Poetry of the highest order has been inspired by it as well as the most sophisticated spiritualities—the two often functioning together, as in the poetry of the world-renowned Sufi poet Rumi. The Qur'an encompasses, in short, a remarkably broad appeal to the human spirit.

The Organization of the Qur'an

The Qur'an is a compilation of the various individual recitings sent down to Muhammad beginning in AD 610 and given their final ordering after the prophet's death in AD 632 by the third caliph, Uthman, following the prophet's wishes. On what principles were the Qur'an's various recitings organized?

At first glance, we're tempted to answer: by no principle at all! The Qur'an seems to be organized in the most confusing way possible. The Qur'an's first *sura* or chapter, called *al-fatihah* or "The Opening" (which we will discuss in the chapter on prayer), is short, just seven lines long. But the second *sura* in order is *al-bakarah* or "The Heifer," and at 286 lines is the Qur'an's longest *sura*. The *sura* placed after *al-bakarah* is the next longest and so on in order of decreasing length until the final *sura,* 114, one of the shortest. Such a principle of organization seems to violate whatever internal or thematic consistency might link one *sura* to another. It violates the chronology of their revelation to Muhammad as well. The longer *suras*—that is, the ones placed earlier in the Qur'an—were actually the last that Muhammad received.

Yet what seems at first an arbitrary ordering principle actually has the effect of reinforcing the Qur'an's special power to command attention. Unlike our Old Testament, which is composed of a vast variety of materials authored by different people and sifted and edited over many centuries, and unlike our New Testament, likewise the product of a variety of sources (though these sources are confined to a much narrower time span), the

Qur'an is regarded by Muslims as a direct revelation given to just one person, Muhammad, over just twenty-two years. And as we've said, its method isn't narrative. It is exhortatory. God speaks to his beloved people directly—warning, haranguing, inspiring them in a language full of poetic turns and rhythmic devices. God's voice is a voice like no other, and it demands to be heard now, without delay. Its "time" is the immediate moment in which its sound erupts in the listener's ear. The listener is not compelled to attend to this voice, but every faculty of reason, emotion and imagination within him or her is addressed and called to account. Nothing less than the ultimate destination of the listener's soul is at stake!

Our Old and New Testaments certainly have moments like this when the voice of the prophet or the psalmist in the Old Testament or the voice of Jesus in the New seem to speak directly to our present condition. The difference is that the entire Qur'an works on this principle. One reason it does so effectively is that the disordering of the *suras* actually aids and abets a principle of immediacy. It may well be that Muhammad chose (under God's inspiration) an apparently confusing order just for the purpose of thwarting the listener's effort to respond to the revelations as one might respond to a story. For the more the revelations seem to tell a story, the less available they are for their primary job of arousing response in the listener's present moment.

The Meccan and Medinan Suras
The possibility that Muhammad chose such a nonnarrative or nonhistorical order deliberately is strengthened by the fact that a historical ordering of the *suras* really is possible. Muslim scholars have worked from Islam's earliest days to establish the ways in which the *suras* fit a chronological and thematic plan. The editors have shown that the *suras* respond to the changing

nature of the challenges confronting Muhammad during the twenty-two years of his prophetic career, from the early days in Mecca right up to some days before his death. By making this demonstration, the editors were not trying to "improve" on the Qur'an but to establish God's gradual refinement of the law revealed to the community as it matured.

The editors of the Qur'an broke the historical ordering of the *suras* down into two categories: the Meccan and the Medinan *suras*. The Meccan *suras*, handed down between AD 610 and the *hijrah* in AD 622, reflect Muhammad's situation in Mecca. The *suras* from this period appeal directly to the conscience and call listeners to reject not only their idolatrous religious practices, but also the arrogant violence of their behavior. The earliest *suras* of this group, appearing in the Qur'an beginning with *sura* 84 until the final *sura*, 114, are remarkably powerful compositions, hymnlike in form and easily memorized. They are designed to rouse listeners from their distractions and obsessions and bring immediately before them the utmost importance of their Islam or self-yielding to God.

By contrast, the Medinan *suras*, handed down starting with the *hijrah* and ending only with Muhammad's death, deal with the exigencies of forming community in Medina among those who have already made their self-yielding. These *suras*, much longer than the Meccan *suras*, tend to be legalistic in content and prosaic in tone. Yet for all the differences between the Meccan and Medinan *suras*, they are united throughout by God's voice: a voice responding in mercy to the beloved people's needs as they struggle to come to self-yielding and then to live out that commitment in a world of time and chance.

PART TWO

COMPARING TEXTS

CHAPTER THREE

WHAT DO WE EACH BELIEVE ABOUT
GOD'S CREATION OF THE UNIVERSE?

Introduction

At the beginning of the book of Genesis, with a rhythm and power that captures the imagination and stirs the heart, God enacts his plan for the universe in six orderly stages. And then, having brought this pyramidal structure into being, God rests on the seventh day.

There is nothing in the Qur'an that resembles this majestic picture of God's creative orderliness in bringing about the universe.

Yet it is not that the Qur'an attempts to achieve such a picture and fails. It is rather that the Qur'an's understanding of creation is different from the one given at the beginning of Genesis.

One difference (a second will be discussed in the next chapter) has to do with the seventh day. The Qur'an insists that God had and has no need to rest. He was always and is always supremely active, supremely creative. Indeed, he never stops creating.

Further, the Qur'an insists that the seventh day, far from a day of rest, is actually the day of creation itself. The seventh day is an eternal present in which human beings and all other created things come into being and pass away. The seventh day sees God's creative power magnificently exerted at each instant. Creation is constant. There is no point at which God sits back, so to speak, and watches while creation goes on of its own accord.

We can see the difference between the Qur'an's and Genesis's understandings of creation in the following excerpt from the Qur'an. Unlike Genesis, the Qur'an makes only a passing allusion to the six days. Instead of building up the account of creation from day one to day six, the Qur'an moves immediately to the present moment, that is, to the present moment of the person listening to or reading the Qur'an's verses, and addresses that person directly.

Unlike Genesis as well, the Qur'an doesn't talk about God. It doesn't, in other words, refer to what God is doing or saying, as if it could see or report on God from the outside. Instead, the Qur'an speaks here and everywhere else in God's own voice, even when, as in the verses that follow until the "we" in verse 58, it speaks in the third person. In Genesis we are made to feel awe at what God has brought into being at the beginning of time. In the Qur'an we are made to feel that creation is an ongoing process that calls us to give unremitting homage to the tireless creator, right here and right now, as we listen to the words of the Qur'an.

The Texts
THE BIBLE
Genesis 1:1, 3, 6, 9, 11, 14–15, 20, 24, 26; 2:1–2

In the beginning when God created the heavens and the earth....Then God said, "Let there be light"; and there was light....

And God said, "Let there be a dome in the midst of the waters, and let it separate the waters from the waters."...

And God said, "Let the waters under the sky be gathered together into one place, and let the dry land appear." And it was so.... Then God said, "Let the earth put forth vegetation: plants yielding seed, and fruit trees of every kind on earth that bear fruit with the seed in it." And it was so....

And God said, "Let there be lights in the dome of the sky to separate the day from the night; and let them be for signs and for seasons and for days and years, and let them be lights in the dome of the sky to give light upon the earth." And it was so....

And God said, "Let the waters bring forth swarms of living creatures, and let birds fly above the earth across the dome of the sky."...

And God said, "Let the earth bring forth living creatures of every kind: cattle and creeping things and wild animals of the earth of every kind." And it was so....

Then God said, "Let us make humankind in our image, according to our likeness; and let them have dominion over the fish of the sea, and over the birds of the air, and over the cattle, and over all the wild animals of the earth, and over every creeping thing that creeps upon the earth."...

Thus the heavens and the earth were finished, and all their multitude. And on the seventh day God finished the work that he had done, and he rested on the seventh day from all the work that he had done.

The Qur'an
sura al-a'raf "The Heights" 7:54–58

7:54For indeed your Lord is God, who created heaven and earth in six days. Then he set himself upon his throne. He covers the night by the day, and the day by the night—each seeks the other in quick succession. The sun and moon and stars bow to his command. Are not that command and the creation his and his alone? Let God be blessed, who cherishes and sustains all created things! [7:55]Call on your Lord in humility and in secret. For God does not love those who go beyond their limits. [7:56]Do not go beyond your bounds on earth now that it has been set in order, but call upon him in fear and longing. For God's mercy is always near for those whose hearts and deeds are beautifully ordered. [7:57]It is he who sends forth the winds as messengers of Good News before his mercy, and as the winds bear along the swollen rain clouds, we give drink to a dead land, causing rain to come down upon it. And we bring forth from it every kind of good fruit. In this way too we will bring forth the dead! Perhaps you will remember? [7:58]And so by the will of its Cherisher the land that is sweet and clean shall bring forth rich growth. But the land that is impure will bring forth nothing but scantiness and bad seed. This is how we explain the signs to a people who are grateful.

GUIDED DISCUSSION QUESTIONS

1. *Is it possible to imagine a universe without the Sabbath?*
In *sura* 7:54, when God tells us that after creating the universe in six days he "set himself upon his throne," we aren't to imagine him resting there. Rather, the throne is a symbol of God's continuing exercise of his creative power. The Qur'an makes the continuing nature of that power explicit in a number of places. Here's one of them: "For it is God that brings things out of nothing and sets them in motion. Then he keeps repeating the process, so that he can reward those who are steadfast in belief and who do good works with justice for all" (*sura yunus* "Jonah" 10:4).

The question for us is: How should we respond to such a deliberate refusal to acknowledge the Sabbath rest? For starters, we need to take seriously the basis of the Qur'an's refusal: that the idea of "rest" seems to diminish and restrict God's creative power. How would we explain our concept of Sabbath to Muslims in a way that could answer their objection? And even more challenging for us may be: Are there ways in which the Muslim objection has merit?

2. Can creation be thought of as moral example?
The Qur'an doesn't deny Genesis's depiction of the creation of the world in six orderly stages. In fact, the Qur'an assumes that its listeners already know about that primordial event from the Hebrew Bible. The Qur'an wants to go instead to a point it believes is too often overlooked: the moral meaning of God's orderly creation. In *sura* 7:54, for example, the fact that the night and the day "seek the other in quick succession" is referred to, not simply to confirm an orderly creative process, but primarily to show us, the Qur'an's audience, the lesson we should draw from that fact. The Qur'an is full of such references to the orderly obedience of the created world to God's *amr* or command. These references are always targeted at human beings with the expectation that they will act according to the *amr* God has given to them as faithfully as the night and the day and all other natural phenomena already do to the *amr* given to them.

Now consider the following question: How often do we as Christians look to natural phenomena to give us keys to our own behavior? What conclusions might we draw from the fact that Muslims do this more regularly than we do?

3. Can we respond to metaphors of the Qur'an the way Muslims do?
As Christians, we're familiar with metaphors—with words or phrases that use one object to refer to another. Prophetic speech is full of metaphors (see Isaiah 2:4, for example, "they shall beat their swords into plowshares, and their spears into pruning hooks…") and so too are the parables of Jesus. The Qur'an is full of metaphors as well. Take *sura* 7:57. There are at least four

levels of meaning at work here. First of all, there is the literal or physical level. God's *amr* or command directs the winds to push the rain clouds toward the dry land in order to water it and to enable it to bear fruit. The winds and the clouds obey God's *amr* or command because they are *muslimun* or "muslim," that is, yielding to his will. (See chapter one, pages 16–19, for an explanation of the meaning of Islam in all its forms.) On the moral level, the winds represent God's mercy ever active in bringing forgiveness, strength and healing to those who truly ask for it. On the spiritual level, the "Good News" refers to the rewards awaiting those at the resurrection of the dead who have received God's mercy. The fourth level is probably the hardest for us to grasp. This level refers to the Qur'an's own way of working on the person listening to its verses. The Arabic word "send forth," for example, is exactly the same word used elsewhere as the "sending forth as messengers" of the Qur'an's own verses. The prophet Muhammad himself is referred to by the same word, as a "messenger." The upshot is that the person listening to these verses can't sit there passively, thinking that the Qur'an here or anywhere is talking about events happening somewhere else, to someone else. The person listening is directly involved in each statement, is in fact its prime target.

With this background in mind, go to the next verse, 7:58, and find where the four levels are at work there as well.

4. *"A people who are grateful" (sura 7:58) as the opposite of "infidels"?*

We sometimes hear the Arabic word that is translated as "infidel" quoted in scary texts by extremist Muslim leaders. The word always seems to be used in that context as a blanket condemnation of all Westerners and of anyone else who might dare to oppose the extremists' ideas or plans. Yet "infidel" has a far richer meaning than as a word to scare and be scared by.

It comes from an Arabic root meaning "cover over, to conceal." As used in the Qur'an, the word means "to cover over God's gifts, to pretend that you never received them." In other words, it is to be "ungrateful." Verse 7:58 illustrates this meaning. God's ceaseless creative activity radiates clear signs of God's power and concern for human beings, but the "ungrateful"–as opposed to "a people who are grateful"–act as if they never saw any such thing. When their ungrateful behavior hardens into a settled denial of God, it takes on the meaning of "faithless." ("Infidel" is actually the old-fashioned form of the same word.)

Is there a Christian equivalent for this way of thinking about "faithlessness"? Knowing as you now do the richer meaning of the word translated "infidel," can you explain how extremists' use of the word distorts that meaning?

CHAPTER FOUR

WHAT DO WE EACH BELIEVE ABOUT GOD'S CREATION OF HUMAN BEINGS?

Introduction

The Qur'an's second difference from Genesis's account of creation has to do with us, with humankind. In Genesis 1:26 creation reaches its peak with the creation of Adam (that is, of humankind) on the sixth day. Human beings occupy creation's pinnacle because "God created humankind [*adama* in Hebrew] in his image, in the image of God he created them" (Genesis 1:27).

By contrast, the Qur'an seems to deny that humans possess such special status. "Surely the creation of heaven and earth is a greater matter than the creation of humankind! But the majority of people know nothing of this" (*sura al-mu'mun* "The Believer" 40:57). But the denial is more apparent than real. The point stressed in the Qur'an is that humankind in its arrogance is only too eager to see itself put on a pedestal. To combat this tendency, the Qur'an ceaselessly reminds us of our high but at the same time humble place in creation. We are bits of clay brought into conscious life through God's creative word. True, we are uniquely endowed with a particular characteristic of God, God's *ruh* or spirit. But this gift gives us no right to behave as if we deserve it or as if we have achieved it by our own merit or as if we can carry it like a trophy.

That is because the *ruh,* or spirit, manifests itself in us as free will—not as a reward but as a responsibility. No other created thing (with the possible exception of the jinn—see page 60 in the next chapter) possesses this divine characteristic. On the one hand, this *ruh* makes humans superior to creatures that are by nature superior to humans. Superior, in the first place, to angels (creatures made of a pure spiritual substance). That is why the angels react with astonishment in *sura* 2:30 when they learn that it is human beings, and not they themselves, whom God has appointed as his "vice-regent" (Arabic *khalifah,* from which English derives the word *caliph*) over creation.

But on the other hand, this very gift of free will, subjected to the baseness of our human nature, will certainly lead to violence and injustice, as the angels are quick to point out. And in *sura* 33:72 we see that the angels' prediction was correct. According to this verse, God offered the vice-regency or "trust" to the heavens, earth and mountains first. The heavens, earth and mountains wisely refused it! Then humankind rushed in where angels too might have feared to tread. The damage done—the "injustice"—is done primarily to ourselves.

And yet, "I know what you do not." These words of God in *sura* 2:30 have been interpreted in many ways. As evidence that angels, themselves possessing no free will, could never understand what God is up to. Or as evidence that God's designs are simply inscrutable, like fate itself. Or as evidence that free will, simply because it is a gift, can never be fully explained or justified rationally. If we Christians think of the gift of free will as a grace (and shouldn't we anyway?), then perhaps we have all the answer possible.

The Texts
THE BIBLE
Genesis 2:4b–7, 18–25

In the day that the LORD God made the earth and the heavens, when no plant of the field was yet in the earth and no herb of the field had yet sprung up—for the LORD God had not caused it to rain upon the earth, and there was no one to till the ground; but a stream would rise from the earth, and water the whole face of the ground—then the LORD God formed man from the dust of the ground, and breathed into his nostrils the breath of life; and the man became a living being....

Then the LORD God said, "It is not good that the man should be alone; I will make him a helper as his partner." So out of the ground the LORD God formed every animal of the field and every bird of the air, and brought them to the man to see what he would call them; and whatever the man called each living creature, that was its name. The man gave names to all cattle, and to the birds of the air, and to every animal of the field; but for the man there was not found a helper as his partner. So the LORD God caused a deep sleep to fall upon the man, and he slept; then he took one of his ribs and he closed up its place with flesh. And the rib that the LORD God had taken from the man he made into a woman and brought her to the man. Then the man said,

"This at last is bone of my bones
    and flesh of my flesh;
this one shall be called Woman,
    for out of Man this one was taken."

Therefore a man leaves his father and his mother and clings to his wife, and they become one flesh. And the man and his wife were both naked, and were not ashamed.

THE QUR'AN

sura al-bakaran, "The Heifer," 2:30–33a

[2:30]For see! Your Cherisher and Sustainer said to the angels, "I will place on earth a vice-regent." The angels said, "Will you indeed place on earth a being who will spread corruption and spill blood, while we angels celebrate your praises and bless your name?" God said, "I know what you do not." [2:31]And God taught Adam the names of all created things. Then God placed these things before the angels and said, "Tell me the names of these things, if you speak the truth." [2:32]The angels said, "All glory is yours. We have no knowledge except what you teach us. Truly, you are perfect in knowledge, perfect in wisdom." [2:33]Then God said, "Now, Adam, tell them their names." When Adam had done so, God said, "Did I not tell you that I know the secrets of heaven and earth? That I know what you conceal and reveal?" [2:34a]And see! We said to the angels, "Bow down to Adam." And they bowed down....

sura al-ahzab, "The Confederate Tribes," 33:72–73

[33:72]For indeed we offered the Trust to the heavens and the earth and the mountains. But they refused to accept it—they were afraid of it. But humankind accepted it. How unjust they were to themselves! How foolhardy! [33:73]So as a result God must punish all who are hypocrites, both men and women, and all who are faithless, both men and women. But God turns toward those men and women who are steadfast in faith. For God is all-forgiving, infinite in mercy.

GUIDED DISCUSSION QUESTIONS

1. *Is humankind not the centerpiece of creation?*

Muslims' apparent refusal to acknowledge humankind as the culminating creative act of God may perplex us. If so, we need to take seriously the basis of the refusal: the belief that looking at ourselves that way simply feeds our pride.

How would we explain to Muslims our understanding of our place in creation (as bearing God's "image") in a way that could answer their objection? In what ways does the Muslim objection have merit?

2. Does it matter that, according to the Qur'an, Eve was not created from Adam's rib?
Our Bible contains two different creation stories. In the first story (Genesis 1–2:4a; see the previous chapter), the word "adam" covers both male and female. "So God created humankind [*adama,* in Hebrew] in his image, in the image of God he created them; male and female he created them" (Genesis 1:27). Humankind is seen right from the start as a pairing. But in the second story of creation (Genesis 2:4b–7, 18–25) a very different picture emerges. Here, the word "adam" becomes the name of the individual male. God feels strongly the absence of Adam's pairing, works to find a suitable "helper" or "partner," and eventually produces Eve from Adam's rib. As for the Qur'an, its understanding of the emergence of the human pair follows Genesis' first story, not its second one. Adam and Eve emerge from a unitary human nature (cf. *sura al-zumar* "The Throngs" 39:6, "We created you from a single self...") and then the one being is turned into a pair. Just how this pairing occurs is not described. The result is clear, however. The primordial pair shares all things equally (even wrongdoing, as discussed in chapter six). One consequence of the Qur'an's emphasis on humankind as a pairing of equals is that it doesn't use the word for the male gender to refer to women as well. We can see this sensitivity to gender in *sura al-ahzab* "The Confederate Tribes" 33:74, where "men and women" are explicitly and separately referred to three times.

Why would such a verse, as well as the absence of the story about Eve's being formed from Adam's rib, allow Muslims to say that the Qur'an doesn't disparage women the way our Bible seems to do? What would you say in answer to this impression Muslims receive from comparing our texts?

3. *Why does Adam name creation?*
Both Genesis and the Qur'an tell us that Adam gave created things their names. But there are at least two significant differences in the way Genesis and the Qur'an imagine that naming.

First, the motives given for the naming of creation are different. According to Genesis 2:18–20, the motive is to enable Adam to locate his true "helper." God brings every living creature before Adam so that Adam can assign each its name. By "name" something much more profound than just a particular word is meant. "Name" refers to the inner nature of the creature. God apparently assumes that among the creatures already existing is one whose inner nature is exactly that of the helper Adam so badly needs. But when the experiment fails and no such creature is found, God has to perform yet another creative act, this time using a piece of Adam's own body. In the Qur'an, by contrast, the motive for the naming has nothing to do with the finding of a helper for Adam. One assumes he already has one. The motive is to demonstrate to the angels the superiority granted to this mere creature of clay by means of God's gift of *ruh,* or spirit.

The second difference has to do with Adam's role in the naming. In the Qur'an, Adam knows the names because God gives them to him. Adam isn't the source of the names. God is. In Genesis, by contrast, God brings all creatures to Adam in order to "see what he would call them." Now Adam is the source of the names, and God waits to see what Adam will say, so as to test and also "bring out" the divine image and likeness.

For us perhaps the best question to ask at this point is not about Adam or the names. It's a question about God and specifically about God's relation to Adam. Two different understandings of the way God relates to Adam are presented by these stories. How would you describe the difference between these ways of relating? Is this difference so great that we are compelled to say that two different Gods are being described here? Or are the Bible and the Qur'an simply looking at the same God in a different way or with a different emphasis?

4. Is there one God or two?
Another window opening on the question, "Do we worship the same God?" is provided by the angels' exchange with God in *sura* 2:30. To the angels' perplexed question, "Will you indeed place on earth a being who will spread corruption and spill blood...?" God replies, "I know what you do not." Compare God's response to the truth about human violence here to his response in Genesis 6:5–8:

> The LORD saw that the wickedness of humankind was great in the earth, and that every inclination of the thoughts of their hearts was only evil continually. And the Lord was sorry that he had made humankind on the earth, and it grieved him to his heart. So the LORD said, "I will blot out from the earth the human beings I have created—people together with animals and creeping things and birds of the air, for I am sorry that I have made them." But Noah found favor in the sight of the LORD.

God reacts very differently in the Qur'an's account and in the biblical account in Genesis to the bitter truth about human violence and faithlessness. What does this difference say about the way Muslims and Christians think about God? Are we each thinking about the same God here?

Another light is thrown on God's decision to put humans in charge of creation by verses 72–73 of *sura* 33. According to these verses, the decision wasn't God's at all but one made by human beings, and it was a bad one! Is the Qur'an contradicting itself? Or are two different aspects of God's plan for us revealed here?

What does it say about the difference in the way we Christians think about our status in creation that we have no story in our Bible that corresponds with verses 33:72–73 of the Qur'an?

5. *Do Christians and Muslims see humankind's relation to the rest of creation in the same way?*
In *sura* 2:30 God declares to the angels that he will "place on earth a vice-regent." The meaning is juridical: that God will deputize human beings to care for the earth in just the same way that God himself would. Compare the Qur'an's account with Genesis 1:26: "Then God said, 'Let us make humankind in our image, according to our likeness; and let them have dominion over the fish of the sea....'"

In one way God is saying the same thing in both places about our relation to the rest of creation. But there is an important difference. What is it?

CHAPTER FIVE

WHAT DO WE EACH BELIEVE ABOUT SATAN?

Introduction

Satan is actually a latecomer to the Bible. He doesn't appear at all in the Old Testament until the time of the Babylonian Exile. Even there, as in the first two chapters of the book of Job, Satan is not portrayed as a force of evil. He is a member of God's court, a kind of appointed prosecutor with the special task of putting decent people like Job to the test, to see whether their virtue is genuine or not.

But as we approach New Testament times, Satan takes on a more sinister aspect. Perhaps influenced by the dualistic beliefs of the surrounding culture, Judaism begins to see Satan in personal terms, acting independently of God and in defiance of him, almost as God's rival in the eternal struggle between good and evil. The New Testament absorbs this influence. Satan tempts Jesus in the desert. He battles with the archangels in the book of Revelation. Christianity, in its effort to understand the meaning of Christ's death and resurrection and to deepen its notion of the power of sin, now identifies Satan with the Serpent in the Garden.

In the Qur'an, Satan doesn't pass through such a development. Right from the start Satan is seen very strictly as humankind's rival and antagonist and tempter, not God's. What's more, he is identified not as an angel (a creature made of a spiritual substance and the highest of God's conscious creations), but as a *jinn,* a creature made of flame, a substance less pure than spirit, but purer than the dried mud from which we humans are formed. Although superior to us in some respects— in powers of invisibility and strength, for example—*jinns* are even more susceptible to wrongdoing than we are.

We see that susceptibility played out in the behavior of Satan (called Iblis) in the following Qur'an excerpt. The excerpt tells the story of God's favoring of Adam (see the Qur'anic excerpt in the previous chapter) from a different angle. There, the emphasis was on Adam's special status and on the angels finally accepting that status by bowing down to the creatures of clay, as God had commanded them. In the following excerpt, the emphasis falls on Satan's refusal to lower himself in such a way, even at God's direct command. While Satan uses this means to defy God and declare his hostility to humankind, he still tends to act like the appointed prosecutor in the book of Job—revealing faithlessness in some human beings, but also confirming the opposite in others. Even in rebellion Satan ends up doing God's work.

The Texts
THE BIBLE
Luke 4:1–13

Jesus, full of the Holy Spirit, returned from the Jordan and was led by the Spirit in the wilderness, where for forty days he was tempted by the devil. He ate nothing at all during those days, and when they were over, he was famished. The devil said to him, "If you are the Son of God, command this stone and become a loaf of bread." Jesus answered him, "It is written, 'One does not live by bread alone.'"

Then the devil led him up and showed him in an instant all the kingdoms of the world. And the devil said to him, "To you I will give their glory and all this authority; for it has been given over to me, and I give it to anyone I please. If you, then, will worship me, it will all be yours." Jesus answered him, "It is written,

'Worship the Lord your God,

and serve only him.'"

Then the devil took him to Jerusalem, and placed him on the pinnacle of the temple, saying to him, "If you are the Son of God, throw yourself down from there, for it is written,

'He will command his angels concerning you,

to protect you',

and

'On their hands they will bear you up,

so that you will not dash your foot against a stone.'"

Jesus answered him, "It is said, 'Do not put the Lord your God to the test.'" When the devil had finished every test, he departed from him until an opportune time.

The Qur'an
sura al-hijr "The Rocky Tract" 15:26–43

15:26We created humankind from clay, molding them from mud. 15:27We created the jinns earlier, from the blazing of a scorching wind. 15:28And see! Your Cherisher and Sustainer said to the angels, "I am about to create humankind from clay, molding them from mud. 15:29And when I have finished shaping them and have breathed my spirit into them, then you must bow down to them in submission." 15:30So the angels bowed down to humankind, all of them together. 15:31Not so Iblis. He refused to join the angels and bow down. 15:32God said, "Iblis! Why is it that you don't bow down?" 15:33Iblis said, "I am not the sort to bow down to a human being, a thing you created from clay, molding them from mud." 15:34God said, "Then off with you, away from here, for you are the sort to be driven off with stones. 15:35And upon you shall be this banishment until the Day of Judgment." 15:36Iblis said, "O my Sustainer and Cherisher, put off this sentence until the Day of Resurrection." 15:37God said, "You will be one of those given a respite 15:38until the Day of the Appointed Time." 15:39Iblis said, "O my Sustainer and Cherisher, since you have led me astray, I will make the wrong look right to those on earth and I will lead them astray, all of them 15:40except those servants of yours whose faith is pure and firm." 15:41God said, "Theirs is a high path, a straight one. 15:42And upon my servants you shall have no authority except upon those who follow you and go astray. 15:43For truly, Hell is the promised place for them."

GUIDED DISCUSSION QUESTIONS

1. "Satan" or "Iblis"?

Some may wonder why Satan was named Iblis in the Qur'anic excerpt printed above. Here are some suggestions to help answer that question. Remember that the names Adam gives things reflect their inner nature. "Iblis" comes from a word meaning "desperation" and "rebellion" and is used only in the passage above (and in another like it) where Iblis is speaking with God. "Satan"—from a word meaning "perversity" and "enmity"—is used whenever his tempting of people is mentioned. Enough said?

2. According to the Qur'an, how great is Satan's power?

First of all, let us sum up the kinds of things Satan does to tempt human beings. Iblis names one of those things in sura 15:39 where he says, "I will make the wrong look right to those on earth." In sura 6:43 he "makes the [evil] things they do look alluring." In sura 3:175 he "causes you to fear his supporters." But perhaps the most telling indication of the kind of power that Satan has over humanity is the verb most often used of him throughout the Qur'an: that he whispers things to people.

Putting all these points together, what would you say is the size of Satan's hold over humankind?

3. *Is the Satan who "whispers" to people and the Satan who tempts Jesus for forty days in the desert the same creature?*
Another way of focusing this question is to compare the behavior of Satan in the Qur'an with the behavior of Satan in Luke 4:1–13. In one way the two Satans are doing the same thing to their intended victims. They are both "making the wrong look right."

Why is it, then, that Satan in Luke's account (and in every other place where he is mentioned in the New Testament) seems so much scarier than the Qur'anic Satan? (A fact for your consideration in answering not only this question but the one following: In Luke, Satan reveals his true motive for tempting Jesus by suggesting that Jesus worship himself rather than God. The Qur'anic Satan whispers a lot of things to people, but never this!)

4. *Would "our" Satan try to have it both ways, as the Muslim Satan does?*
Often in those many instances in which the Qur'an depicts the Day of Judgment, Satan's behavior on that Day is described. Here's one such place, from *sura al-hashr* "Exile" 59:16:

> The hypocrites are like Satan when he says to humankind, "Go ahead, disbelieve, be ungrateful to God." For when humankind disbelieves, Satan says on the Day of Judgment, "As for me, I am free of you. I fear God, the Cherisher and Sustainer of the worlds!"

Needless to say, God isn't taken in by this disclaimer because in the very next verse Satan is thrown into the fire of hell. Yet the people he has seduced aren't thereby let off from punishment. They are thrown in too!

What attitude toward God does Satan display in this scene (and in others like it) where at the last minute he absolves himself of all responsibility for tempting humankind? What attitude does he display toward humanity? Based on your answers, how would you describe the moral character of the Qur'anic Satan?

Would you expect such behavior from Satan as we know him from the New Testament? Why or why not?

5. Is this sympathy for the devil?
For the great majority of Muslims, Satan is a figure to be shunned and repelled. Muslim prayers begin with a formula that says: "I ask protection from Satan the deceiver, the rejected one." One of the customs during the *hajj* or pilgrimage to Mecca is to throw stones at a pillar representing Satan. Yet among certain Sufis or Muslim mystics there has grown up a tradition of respect for Satan, based especially on his dialogue with God. Here is one such story:

> [Iblis] was told: "Bow down!" He said, "[to] no other!" He was asked [by God], "Even if you receive my curse?" He said, "It does not matter. I have no way to an other-than-you. I am an abject lover."[1]

Sufis' respect for Iblis is based on what they see as the real motive behind Iblis's refusal. His real motive wasn't defiance. It was fidelity to the principle of God's *tawhid* or uniqueness. So committed was Iblis to worshipping God and God alone that he could not, even at God's command, bow down to anything or anyone else. That would be an act of idolatry! The purity of the commitment is actually verified by Iblis's willingness to suffer God's "curse" as a result. In this way, Iblis comes to serve as a model of selfless devotion to God, of a love so pure that neither the prospect of reward (heaven) or of punishment (hell) can deflect it.

The question for us Christians: Why is such "sympathy for the devil" unthinkable? What prevents us from seeing Satan in any kind of favorable light?

NOTE

1. Michael A. Sells, ed., *Early Islamic Mysticism: Sufi, Qur'an, Mi'raj, Poetic and Theological Writings* (Mahwah, N.J.: Paulist, 1996), p. 274.

CHAPTER SIX

WHAT DO WE EACH BELIEVE ABOUT ADAM AND EVE IN THE GARDEN?

Introduction

Both the Bible and the Qur'an are repetitive.

We've already talked about the two creation stories in Genesis, and there are many other repeated stories in the Old Testament as well. In the New Testament the story of Christ's ministry on earth is told not once but four times. None of these repetitions is word for word, however. The repetitions reflect different understandings of the basic materials by the different storytellers and their communities. Their separate versions were over time woven into the larger fabric of the two Testaments.

Yet repetition plays a different role in the Qur'an than it does in the Bible. The difference is due in part to the fact that the Qur'anic revelations came only to one person over a relatively short period of time. It's due in part also to the difference in the way the Qur'an addresses its readers. The Qur'an consists, according to Muslims, of the separate *qur'an*'s, or "recitings," of God's very words. And those words are always words of warning—"wake-up calls," we would say. So when the Qur'an retells a story, it does so in order to shake its readers out of their inattentiveness and moral sluggishness. Often the retellings amount to little more than allusions. The main point is to rouse its readers from spiritual sloth and slumber by casting a familiar story in a new and often surprising form.

Take the two versions of Adam and Eve compared with the Bible's single account. The first Qur'anic version, from *sura al-bakara* or "The Heifer," is meant to reawaken human beings to God's power over all creation, beginning with God's first human creation, Adam and Eve. The second Qur'anic version, from *sura al-a'raf* or "The Heights," focuses more narrowly on the way human beings, beginning with Adam and Eve, have actually responded to God's efforts to awaken them. That's why the second version gives more details, especially in the form of dialogue, not only between Satan and Adam and Eve and then between God and Adam and Eve, but also between God and the "Children of Adam," that is, us!

That fact—that God ends up the second version by address-ing humanity directly—says a lot about the Qur'an's special power. Unlike the Bible, the Qur'an is constantly "in your face." Not in a bullying way, but insistently. We are not allowed to look at any fact or story, including Adam and Eve's story, from a distance. The peril Adam and Eve put themselves in and their narrow escape is the peril we find ourselves in right now, as we sleepily find ourselves roused by the call of the Qur'an.

Christians and Muslims define the peril differently, how-ever. The difference shows up in the different way the Qur'an and the Bible tell the story of Adam and Eve. According to the Qur'an, Adam and his mate—it's clearly Eve, though she isn't mentioned—"slip" from the Garden. Their departure is a punish-ment, yes. But it's far less catastrophic than what happens to Adam and Eve in Genesis. And the consequences are very differ-ent too. In the Qur'anic account, no sooner are they out of the

Garden than God forgives them! (See the following *sura* 2:37.) These two observations alone give us lots to think about as we compare and contrast Muslim and Christian attitudes toward human sinfulness.

The Texts
THE BIBLE
Genesis 3

Now the serpent was more crafty than any other wild animal that the LORD God had made. He said to the woman, "Did God say, 'You shall not eat from any tree in the garden'?" The woman said to the serpent, "We may eat of the fruit of the trees in the garden; but God said, "You shall not eat of the fruit of the tree that is in the middle of the garden, nor shall you touch it, or you shall die.'" But the serpent said to the woman, "You will not die; for God knows that when you eat of it your eyes will be opened, and you will be like God, knowing good and evil." So when the woman saw that the tree was good for food, and that it was a delight to the eyes, and that the tree was to be desired to make one wise, she took of its fruit and ate; and she also gave some to her husband, who was with her, and he ate. Then the eyes of both were opened, and they knew that they were naked; and they sewed fig leaves together and made loincloths for themselves.

They heard the sound of the LORD God walking in the garden at the time of the evening breeze, and the man and his wife hid themselves from the presence of the LORD God among the trees of the garden. But the LORD God called to the man, and said to him, "Where are you?" He said, "I heard the sound of you in the garden, and I was afraid, because I was naked; and I hid myself." He said, "Who told you that you were naked? Have you eaten from the tree of which I commanded you not to eat?" The man said, "The woman whom you gave to be with me, she gave me fruit from the tree, and I ate." Then the LORD God said to the woman, "What is this that you have done?" The woman said, "The serpent tricked me, and I ate." The LORD God said to the serpent,

> "Because you have done this,
>> cursed are you among all animals
>> and among all wild creatures;
> upon your belly you shall go,
>> and dust you shall eat
>> all the days of your life.
> I will put enmity between you and the woman,
>> and between your offspring and hers;
> he will strike your head,
>> and you will strike his heel."

To the woman he said,

> "I will greatly increase your pangs in childbearing;
>> in pain you shall bring forth children,
> yet your desire shall be for your husband,
>> and he shall rule over you."

And to the man he said,

> "Because you have listened to the voice of your wife,
>> and have eaten of the tree
> about which I commanded you,
>> 'You shall not eat of it,'
> cursed is the ground because of you;
>> in toil you shall eat of it all the days of your life;
> thorns and thistles it shall bring forth for you;
>> and you shall eat the plants of the field.
> By the sweat of your face
>> you shall eat bread
> until you return to the ground,
>> for out of it you were taken;
> you are dust,
>> and to dust you shall return."

The man named his wife Eve, because she was the mother of all living. And the LORD God made garments of skins for the man and for his wife, and clothed them.

Then the LORD God said, "See, the man has become like one of us, knowing good and evil; and now, he might reach out his hand and take also from the tree of life, and eat, and live forever"—therefore the LORD God sent him forth from the garden of Eden, to till the ground from which he was taken. He drove out the man; and at the east of the garden of Eden he placed the cherubim, and a sword flaming and turning to guard the way to the tree of life.

THE QUR'AN
sura al-bakarah "The Heifer" 2:35–39

2:35[God is speaking, in the first person plural.] We said: "Adam, live with your mate in Paradise and eat of its fruits to your hearts' content wherever you want. But never approach this tree or you will both go into the dark, harming yourselves and others." 2:36But Satan made them slip from the Garden and leave the state they had been in. "Go down from here, all three of you," we said. "Be enemies to each other. The earth for a while will provide you a place and comfort." 2:37Then Adam learned words from his Lord, and so his Lord turned toward him and relented. For God is the One Who Turns, the Merciful. 2:38"Go down from here, all three of you," we said. "When my guidance is revealed to you two and your offspring, the ones that follow that guidance will have nothing to fear or regret. 2:39But those who are ungrateful and say that our signs of mercy are lies, they will become companions in the fire, and there they will live forever."

sura al-a'araf "The Heights" 7:19–27

7:19[God is still speaking, now in the third person singular.] To Adam he said: "Live with your mate in Paradise, and eat of any

71

fruit you want to: but never approach this tree or you both go into the dark, harming yourselves and others." 7:20Then Satan began to whisper suggestions to them, so as to reveal to them their shameful parts that were hidden from them before. He said: "The only reason your Lord forbids you this tree, is to prevent you from becoming angels or other such beings that live forever." 7:21And he swore to them both that he was their confidant, their adviser. 7:22So by trickery he caused them to go astray. When they tasted of the tree, their shameful parts were revealed to them, and they began to sew together the leaves of the Garden over their bodies. And their Lord called out to them: "Didn't I forbid you that tree, and tell you that Satan was your sworn enemy?" [This piece of the story is given in *sura ta-ha* 20:117.] 7:23They said: "Lord, we have done wrong to our souls. Pardon us and have mercy on us, because otherwise we'll surely end up among the lost." 7:24God said: "Go down from here, all three of you, and may your descendants be enemies to each other. The earth will for a while provide you a place and comfort. 7:25There you two and your descendants shall live and there you shall die, and from there you shall be taken out again and raised up to life."

7:26Children of Adam! We have given you clothing to cover your shameful parts, as well as to make you beautiful. But the clothing of righteousness—that is the best. These are examples of our signs to you. Who knows? Maybe these signs will wake you up and remind you of our mercy. 7:27O Children of Adam! Don't let Satan seduce you as he did your parents when he caused them to leave the Garden. He stripped them of their clothing to expose their shameful parts. For he and his gang spy upon you from a place where you can't see them. We made the Satans to be confidants only to those who have no faith.

GUIDED DISCUSSION QUESTIONS

1. A Qur'anic "Fall"?

In *sura* 2:35 Adam and his mate "slip from the Garden and leave the state they had been in."

What does this wording—so different from the language used in Genesis 3 and in later interpretations of the "Fall"—say about the Qur'an's view of the depth of human sinfulness? Compared to the traditional Christian judgment of Adam and Eve's behavior in Genesis 3, how badly did Adam and Eve go astray in the Qur'anic account?

2. Why is there no Tree of Good and Evil in the Qur'anic Garden?

The Qur'an speaks of only one Tree in the Garden, the Tree of Life (see *sura* 7:20). The Qur'an says nothing about the Tree of Good and Evil, from which Adam and Eve eat in the biblical account—the Tree whose fruit makes Adam and Eve "like one of us," i.e., like God himself.

Why do you suppose the Qur'an is silent about the Tree of Good and Evil? What does the silence say about the Qur'an's understanding of the depth of the evil humanity is capable of? How is that understanding different from the Bible's?

3. Does "salvation" make sense to Muslims?

Even before they're forced to leave the Garden in both Qur'anic accounts, Adam and Eve, waking from their error, beg God's forgiveness—and receive it!

Why would this telling of the story make it very difficult for Muslims to understand what we Christians mean by "salvation history"—or indeed by "salvation" itself?

4. Was Adam's mate a temptress?

Think about the difference between Eve's role in responding to the serpent's temptation in the Genesis account and the role of Adam's mate (literally, "paired complement") in the temptation account in the Qur'an. You also might want to revisit question 2 at the end of chapter four, where there is further basis for comparing the Qur'an's and the Bible's understanding of women's role at and in creation.

Can you see why the Qur'anic verses cited in this chapter could reinforce Muslims' impression that the biblical accounts of Eve tend to disparage women, while the Qur'anic accounts stress her equal status with Adam? How could you go about correcting that impression?

5. *Original sin: How does this belief of ours look to Muslims?*
Pretend that a Muslim friend asked you to explain to him or her the concept of original sin.

Based on your readings and reflections so far, would you say that you'd have an easy time doing this?

CHAPTER SEVEN

WHAT DO WE EACH BELIEVE ABOUT THE ANNUNCIATION TO MARY?

Introduction

The topic of the next several chapters—the identity of Jesus and the meaning of his mission—will put our patience and forbearance to the test. The problem for us is that while the Qur'an never looks at Jesus with anything less than admiration, it most emphatically does not view Jesus as God's son. We Christians might feel more comfortable if the Qur'an had ignored Jesus altogether or even if it had spoken disparagingly about him. Then, at least, we could mount a vigorous defense of him. But to see Jesus honored as a prophet and as a prophet only is to find ourselves in a position of rivalry with Islam. Christians and Muslims cannot both be correct about Jesus.

Does that fact, however, necessarily mean that the mistaken party's love of Jesus (and of course we Christians identify the mistaken party with Muslims) is worthless or even a form of dishonor to him? For centuries our Christian ancestors thought so. To them, Islam—which they called "Muhammadanism"—was a heresy originated by Muhammad himself and stubbornly perpetuated by subsequent Muslim generations. The Qur'an's refusal to accept Jesus as Son of God seemed to earlier Christians an unforgivable act of defiance, while the Qur'an's honoring of Jesus merely as a prophet seemed an unwelcome tribute, even a form of mockery.

We Catholic Christians face a parallel difficulty in talking with Muslims about Mary. As in the question of Jesus' divinity, we find ourselves in a position of rivalry. Muslims eagerly point out that they love Mary also and that she is actually mentioned more often in the Qur'an than she is in the Gospels. One whole *sura* of the Qur'an bears her name—an honor given to no other woman. In fact, she is the only woman whose name actually occurs in the Qur'an. And she is honored above all women by being selected by God to bear a son through the Holy Spirit. The Virgin Birth is as much a Muslim belief as it is a Christian one. Yet the son to whom she gives birth is a prophet, not God.

Even though Vatican II overturned the church's centuries-old denunciation of Islam, we are still uneasy about how to talk with Muslims about Jesus and Mary. Talk we must, however, because belief in Jesus' divinity is central to our Christian faith, while belief in Jesus as prophet is incumbent on every Muslim. Yet here we meet a perplexing asymmetry. Muslims don't share our need to talk about Jesus. Jesus is for them one of the great prophets, to be sure. Yet Muslim faith in God does not revolve around Jesus. Muslim faith revolves around the prophet whose advent the Qur'an says Jesus predicted, the prophet Muhammad himself. It is hard for us to accept a situation where Jesus is a subordinate figure, though an honored one. And because Jesus plays a subordinate role, Mary does too—despite all the special honor given to her in the Qur'an.

We Catholic Christians, in our conversations with Muslims about Jesus and Mary, face the task of restraining our competitive instincts and of listening to what Muslims have to say. Are our imaginations free enough to allow us to see Jesus and Mary through Muslim eyes? We have at least grown beyond the church's previous suspicion that Muslims are in any way mocking the Blessed Mother and her Son.

The Texts
THE BIBLE
Luke 1:26–38

In the sixth month the angel Gabriel was sent by God to a town in Galilee called Nazareth, to a virgin engaged to a man whose name was Joseph, of the house of David. The virgin's name was Mary. And he came to her and said, "Greetings, favored one! The Lord is with you." But she was much perplexed by his words and pondered what sort of greeting this might be. The angel said to her, "Do not be afraid, Mary, for you have found favor with God. And now, you will conceive in your womb and bear a son, and you will name him Jesus. He will be great, and will be called the Son of the Most High, and the Lord God will give to him the throne of his ancestor David. He will reign over the house of Jacob forever, and of his kingdom there will be no end." Mary said to the angel, "How can this be, since I am a virgin?" The angel said to her, "The Holy Spirit will come upon you, and the power of the Most High will overshadow you; therefore the child to be born will be holy; he will be called Son of God. And now, your relative Elizabeth in her old age has also conceived a son; and this is the sixth month for her who was said to be barren. For nothing will be impossible with God." Then Mary said, "Here am I, the servant of the Lord; let it be with me according to your word." Then the angel departed from her.

THE QUR'AN
sura imran "Imran" 3:35–38, 42–51

[3:35]Behold! The wife of Imran, Mary's mother-to-be, said, "O my Cherisher and Sustainer, I solemnly vow to dedicate to your service the child now in my womb. I ask you to accept this offering, for you hear all things, you know all things." [3:36]Afterward, when she had been delivered of the child, she said, "O my Cherisher and Sustainer, I have brought forth a female child!" Of course God knew very well the child's gender. "Yet," she said, "isn't a female child just as acceptable to you as a male child?" I have named her Mary, and I commend her and her own children to your protection from Satan the deceiver."

3:37God was most pleased to receive the child from her mother. He caused the child to flourish in purity and beauty and gave her over to the care of Zechariah.

3:38Each time that Zechariah came to visit Mary in her chamber, he found her supplied with all kinds of provisions. He said, "O Mary, where do these bounties come from?" She answered, "They are from God. For God lavishes bounty on whomever he pleases." 3:39Right then and there Zechariah prayed to God, "O my Cherisher and Sustainer, grant me as well a child that is pure. For you hear and answer our prayers...."

3:42Behold! The angels said, "O Mary, know that God has preferred you and has purified you—choosing you from among the women of all the worlds. 3:43O Mary, be faithful to your Cherisher and Sustainer. Bow down to the ground and to the waist along with those who do the same."

3:44This, O Muhammad, is taken from the prophecies of hidden things which we grant to you through inspiration. For you were not there with the priests as they cast lots with their arrowshafts to see who among them would win the privilege of caring for Mary. Nor were you with them when they wrangled over the honor.

3:45Behold! The angels said, "O Mary, know that God has brought glad tidings to you of a Word from him. The child's name shall be 'Isa the Messiah, the son of Mary, a prophet honored in this world and the world to come, and one of those closest to God. 3:46He shall speak to humankind from infancy to his years of maturity, and he shall be counted among the righteous."

3:47She said in reply, "O my Cherisher and Sustainer, how can it happen that I should bear a son when no man has ever touched me?" Then he said, "Like this—God creates whatever he wills. When God gives a command, all he has to do is say 'Be!'– and it is!"

sura maryam "Mary" 19:16–21

19:16 Remember what it says in the Book how Mary, when she withdrew from her family to a private eastern space to the east, 19:17how she placed a screen to protect herself from intrusion and we sent down to her our own Spirit who appeared before her as a man in every way. 19:18She said, "I seek protection against you from the most gracious God. You will not harm me if you have respect for God."

19:19He said, "Don't be afraid, Mary. I am only a messenger from your Cherisher and Sustainer, bringing you news that you will bear a pure son."

19:20She said in reply, "How can I bear a son when no man has ever touched me? And when I am not unchaste?"

19:21He answered, "Like this–Your Cherisher and Sustainer says, 'This is easy for me. For our intention is to make him a Sign to humankind and a Mercy from us. It is a matter ordained.'"

sura al-tahrim "Prohibition" 66:12

66:12And another example of those who believe was Mary, the daughter of Imran, who guarded her chastity–she is the one into whom we breathed our Spirit, and she upheld the truth of the Word and of the Revelations of her Cherisher and Sustainer and so she is numbered among the Devout ones."

GUIDED DISCUSSION QUESTIONS

1. Do Muslims honor Mary more than we do?

This may seem an almost offensive question to ask, but consider the facts. In Luke's account, Mary comes from a poor peasant village in Galilee. By contrast, the Qur'an raises Mary's social status by treating her as a consecrated virgin and by turning her into the special ward of the prophet Zechariah, here seen not as an obscure Galilean figure but as a powerful member of the temple clergy.

Should we be offended by such a retelling of "our" story, even though by means of it the honor given Mary is increased?

2. Is Joseph's absence from Jesus' and Mary's story a slight? Or is it another honor given Mary—and Jesus too?
Joseph is notable in the Qur'an by his absence.

Should we Christians take offense at his erasure from the Holy Family? Or should we see his absence as Muslims do, as a way of protecting Mary's honor from the rumor of fraud and adultery?

3. Is Mary the same person in Luke's and in the Qur'an's account of the Annunciation?
Aside from her different social status in the two accounts, Mary in Luke and Mary in the Qur'an seem to be the same person. In both scriptures she is a virgin singled out for a unique divine intervention. She reacts to this news in approximately the same way, first with wonder and concern and then with acquiescence. (The acquiescence is directly stated in Luke; it is implied in the Qur'an.)

Yet if Mary's identity is indelibly shaped by the son she bears, how can it be the same person who bears a prophet—however miraculously—and the Son of God (Luke 1:35)? How does she become different as a result of Luke's and the Qur'an's statements about the identity of her son?

CHAPTER EIGHT

WHAT DO WE EACH BELIEVE ABOUT THE BIRTH OF JESUS?

Introduction

If we Christians feel uneasy about the Qur'an's account of Jesus' birth and of its immediate aftermath, we should remember that Muslims will probably be feeling equally uneasy about the biblical account of the "same" events. The only solution is to listen in patience to what the other has to say. Such patience will be particularly difficult for Christians since the Qur'an explicitly singles Christians out for chastisement. What we regard as the central meaning of Jesus' birth—that through it God became human—is looked at by the Qur'an as an act of idolatry (see the following *sura maryam* 19:34–37)! Can our Christian patience receive such a blow without snapping?

An angry or even a dismissive reaction on our part to the Qur'anic chastisement might cause us to look with suspicion at the entire account of Jesus' birth as the Qur'an tells it. Mary's flight all alone into what seems to be the Arabian desert, the voice speaking to her from beneath the palm tree, and, later, the newly born Jesus' defense of his mother before the townspeople—these events may seem simply absurd, even offensive, like magical happenings in a fairy tale. Yet Matthew's and Luke's renderings of the story contain elements that could uncharitably be called fabulous as well. Consider the star standing still over Bethlehem, for example, or even the appearance of the Magi seemingly out of nowhere. And if we complain that the Qur'an tells the story of Jesus' birth very differently from the way Matthew and Luke tell it, we have to acknowledge that Matthew's and Luke's accounts do not agree on details. For example, Jesus according to Matthew is born in a house; according to Luke he is born in a stable. This difference as well as others suggest that various versions of the story of Jesus' birth arose in the early tradition. The New Testament and the Qur'an simply reflect this variety.

As for the Qur'anic account itself, a calm appraisal reveals that, different as it might be from the New Testament accounts, it still manages to treat mother and child with the utmost respect. Mary's flight into what seems to be a harsh and lonely landscape (reminiscent of the barren areas in the Arabian desert) is seen as a natural if desperate reaction by a girl who is pregnant and without a husband. Fear of scandal and of capital punishment drive her forth from her sanctuary; in Luke's account it is the Roman census that sends her forth. (Fear of scandal and its consequences play a larger role in Matthew's account; see Matthew 1:18–25.) Once strengthened by the angelic voice, Mary assumes a new tone of authority. Unsupported and unprotected by males, she stands forth ready to defend herself from them, should they besiege her. She apparently gives birth to her child all by herself. Hardly a picture of female weakness!

The infant Jesus' defense of her before the townspeople has its own power and point, once we get over its strangeness. Instead of directly answering the townspeople's implied accusation that his mother is a fornicator and that he himself is illegitimate, Jesus calmly asserts his full adult identity, as if his life had already been lived in advance. Evidently this was enough to stifle the accusation, to protect his mother from disgrace and punishment and to clarify his own role as a prophet uniquely created by God.

But what is perhaps most curious about the infant Jesus' speech to the townspeople is that it sets up a parallel with the proclamation in Luke. Both Luke and the Qur'an speak with wonder of Jesus' birth by a virgin. Where they differ is that in the New Testament the angels, the heavens and the shepherds all testify to the infant Jesus' glory, while in the Qur'an it is the infant Jesus who testifies—to his mother's chastity, as validated by his own prophetic destiny.

The Texts

THE BIBLE

Luke 2:3–20

All went to their own towns to be registered. Joseph also went from the town of Nazareth in Galilee to Judea, to the city of David called Bethlehem, because he was descended from the house and family of David. He went to be registered with Mary, to whom he was engaged and who was expecting a child. While they were there, the time came for her to deliver her child. And she gave birth to her firstborn son and wrapped him in bands of cloth, and laid him in a manger, because there was no place for them in the inn.

In that region there were shepherds living in the fields, keeping watch over their flock by night. Then an angel of the Lord stood before them, and the glory of the Lord shone around them, and they were terrified. But the angel said to them, "Do not be afraid; for see—I am bringing you good news of great joy for all the people: to you is born this day in the city of David a

Savior, who is the Messiah, the Lord. This will be a sign for you: you will find a child wrapped in bands of cloth and lying in a manger." And suddenly there was with the angel a multitude of the heavenly host, praising God and saying,

"Glory to God in the highest heaven,
    and on earth peace among those whom he favors!"

When the angels had left them and gone into heaven, the shepherds said to one another, "Let us go now to Bethlehem and see this thing that has taken place, which the Lord has made known to us." So they went with haste and found Mary and Joseph, and the child lying in the manger. When they saw this, they made known what had been told them about this child; and all who heard it were amazed at what the shepherds told them. But Mary treasured all these words and pondered them in her heart. The shepherds returned, glorifying and praising God for all they had heard and seen, as it had been told them.

THE QUR'AN
sura maryam "Mary" 19:22–37

19:22So Mary conceived 'Isa. Then she withdrew once more to an even more remote place. 19:23Her birth-pangs brought her to the shade of a date palm tree. She cried out, "Oh, how much better if I had died before this. How much better to be a thing lost and forgotten." 19:24Just then a voice cried out from beneath the palm tree, "Don't despair, Mary, for your Cherisher and Sustainer has made a stream flow at your feet. 19:25And shake loose some dates from the palm tree. 19:26It will drop fresh ripe dates down for you. Eat and drink and refresh yourself. And if you see any male stranger, say, 'I have made a vow to the Merciful One to undergo a fast. Nor shall I speak this day to any human being.'"

19:27Once 'Isa was born, Mary brought him to her people, carrying the babe in her arms. The townspeople said, "Oh Mary, what a strange thing you've brought home! 19:28Oh daughter of

Aaron, your father never chased after prostitutes, nor was your mother a whore." [19:29]But instead of defending herself, Mary pointed at her child. The townspeople said, "How are we supposed to talk with a child in a cradle?" [19:30]But the child spoke up. "Hear this," he said. "I am a servant of God. God has given me his message and has made me a prophet. [19:31]He has made me blessed wherever I go, and he has commanded me to be faithful to prayer and almsgiving as long as I live. [19:32]He has made me gentle and just with my mother, neither bossy nor irritable. [19:33]So peace [salaam] is with me from the day of my birth to the day of my death till the day I shall be raised to life."

[19:34]Such a man was 'Isa, son of Mary. This is the truth, about which the various Christian sects vainly dispute. [19:35]For it is not fitting that God should beget a son. Glory to God! When God decrees a matter, he only has to say of it, "Be!"—and it exists. [19:36]Remember that God is my Cherisher and Sustainer and yours as well. So worship him and him alone. [19:37]But the Christian sects differ rancorously among each other. Woe to the unbelievers at the Reckoning on that Terrible Day!

GUIDED DISCUSSION QUESTIONS

1. *Is the voice from beneath the palm tree magical or angelic?* Christian readers need to come to their own conclusions about Mary's second "withdrawal," this time into the desert.

Does the voice that comforts Mary in the Qur'anic account trivialize the event by seeming to turn it into a tall tale? Or is this voice meant to express heaven and earth's approval of Mary? If so, what are they approving her for? And how are the qualities referred to or suggested in this *sura* like and unlike the qualities displayed by Luke's account of Mary?

2. *To what extent do Mary in the New Testament and Mary in the Qur'an understand who their infant sons are?*
The various Gospel accounts of Mary's relation with Jesus provide rich material for speculation. We Christians over the ages have agreed that their relation was extraordinarily intimate and have expressed this intimacy in our spirituality, liturgy, iconography and theology. By contrast, the Qur'an provides far fewer details on which to base such speculation. One such detail emerges in the passage given, however—the statement that after the townspeople had made their insinuation about Mary's bad behavior, "Mary, instead of defending herself, pointed at her child."

What does Mary's apparently unhesitating wordless reaction tell us about her understanding of who her son is? How do you suppose she gained this understanding? Why do you suppose the Qur'an tells us nothing about how she gained it?

What happens when one compares the Qur'anic Mary's assumed understanding of her son with Mary's understanding in Luke 2:19: "But Mary treasured all these words and pondered them in her heart"? Could it be said that the New Testament Mary's understanding took longer to develop than the Qur'anic Mary's? Why would there be such a difference?

3. *Christian divisiveness and wrangling: as much a scandal then as now?*
While the Qur'an often states that Christians deserve special commendation for their fidelity to God, it states just as often that they are to be shunned and mistrusted because of all their disputing among themselves. What the Qur'an seems to be referring to is Christian argumentativeness over the nature of God, one sect taking one position, another sect taking a rival one. To put the Qur'an's chastisement in context, we need to remember that disputes about the nature of God had torn the

church apart in earlier centuries. The disputes mostly turned on the identity of Jesus. Arianism held Jesus to be a creature, albeit nearly divine. Modalism held him to be a phase of God's unicity. Monophysites considered that his human nature was swallowed up by his divine nature. Nestorians taught that while Jesus possessed both human and divine natures, those natures were not unified in one Person. These are only a few of the views held to be heretical by the time of the fourth Ecumenical Council at Chalcedon, near what is now Istanbul, in AD 451. One hundred and sixty years later, these disputes were still simmering, especially in remote areas of the world—such as the Arabian peninsula—not under the direct control of a Christian monarch.

How might this sketch of the situation help us understand why the Qur'an would want to set the record straight, according to its own understanding? Why it would say so forcefully, "Such a man was 'Isa, son of Mary. This is the truth, about which the various Christian sects vainly dispute"? Naturally we Catholic Christians don't agree with the Qur'an's conclusion. Does our disagreement prevent us from sympathizing with those who found the disputing itself scandalous behavior?

4. *Why does the Qur'an reject the idea that Jesus is God's son?*
Think about the logic of the following Qur'anic lines: "For it is not fitting that God should beget a son. Glory to God! When God decrees a matter, he only has to say of it, 'Be!'—and it exists."

What idea about "begetting a son" is the Qur'an objecting to? How is this use of "begetting" different from its use in the Nicene Creed that Catholic Christians recite every Sunday at Mass ("...begotten, not made...")? How would you explain our meaning of "beget" to a Muslim?

What about the apparent finality of the logic underlying the third line beginning "When God decrees a matter..."? What presumed error does this logic answer? Do you find that you as a Christian actually espouse the erroneous logic corrected here?

To what extent is the Qur'anic chastisement based on misconceptions? Is there room here for at least the beginning steps of agreement between Muslims and Christians, even in the face of what looks like an unequivocal Qur'anic rejection of the Christian core belief in Jesus as God's Son?

CHAPTER NINE

WHAT DO WE EACH BELIEVE ABOUT THE CRUCIFIXION AND RESURRECTION?

Introduction

Let's say we Christians manage not to clash with Muslims over our differing interpretations of the Annunciation. Can we breathe easy and believe that we're in the clear, that no further conflicts await to trip us up? No, alas, we can't. A thornier path lies ahead. This is the path that leads to Calvary.

What actually happened on Calvary? This is not a simple question, even for Christians. The fact is that each of the Gospel accounts of Jesus' crucifixion tells the story a little differently. Yet different as the accounts are, all agree that Jesus really did die on the cross. All describe the crucifixion and the immediate events that led up to it in great detail as if to drive home the point that Jesus' death took place in actual fact. This insistence on the factuality of Jesus' death highlights the glory of what happened three days later: Jesus' own resurrection and his promise of resurrection to all who believe.

Yet we know that right from the start that there arose conflicting interpretations of what happened on Calvary. Initially, many people, among them Romans and Jews, while agreeing with Christians that Jesus died on the cross, vigorously denied his resurrection. They held that Jesus died like any other executed criminal, and that was that. At the other extreme, the apocryphal gospels as well as the writings of the Gnostics in the second and third centuries AD denied both that Jesus died and that he rose again. According to these documents, either a lookalike died in Jesus' stead or else Jesus' body only appeared to die. These interpretations, later branded as heretical, were attempts to rescue God from contamination by mere human flesh. The division between heaven and earth was so great that God would never have sunk so low as to become one with flesh, as orthodox Christians claimed.

The Qur'an, like the apocryphal gospels and the Gnostic writings, also rejects the Christian assertion that Jesus died on the cross. Yet the Qur'an's reasons for doing so are opposed to Gnosticism's. Gnosticism's antipathy to the idea of Jesus' death on the cross reflects a dualistic belief in the absolute division between the pure realm of the spirit and the muddy pollution of flesh. The Qur'an, by contrast, upholds the physical world as God's direct and ongoing creation and is suspicious of ascetical or spiritualizing tendencies that seek to turn the human body into a symbol of pollution and sin.

Nevertheless, for all of its difference from Gnosticism on this point, the Qur'an seems to employ Gnostic-like arguments to support its assertion that Jesus did not die on the cross. These arguments aren't made at any length. The truth is that the Qur'an is simply vague on the question of what happened on Calvary. This vagueness in some ways makes dialogue with Muslims harder than if the Qur'an had explicitly advanced an opposing view. We Christians could then have risen up in opposition. But the Qur'an passes over the events on Calvary in a single verse, and it treats the argument over those events as little more than a kind of quicksand of bad reasoning and fanaticism. What's more, the Qur'an inserts its brief treatment at the end of a list of the sins, not of Christians, but of Jews. According to the Qur'an, the only point of mentioning the crucifixion of Jesus at all is to use it as a culminating example of the Jews' stubborn self-centeredness. The Jews, says the Qur'an, actually had the effrontery to claim that they had been able to kill a prophet sent by God! Would a merciful God have allowed any of his prophets to suffer such a miserable end? God's prophets might be rejected, just as Muhammad was rejected initially by the Meccans. But ultimately they and their cause must be vindicated. Crucifixion, in Muslims' eyes, violates the dignity of God's cause.

As for us Christians, we are never mentioned in the Qur'an's fleeting reference to the Crucifixion. If we are referred to at all, we are referred to obliquely, as among those who keep disputing about what happened at Calvary. Otherwise, the central event of Christian faith—the Paschal Mystery—is passed over in silence.

It is hard for us to have our beliefs seemingly brushed off in this way. Is it possible for us not to take offense? Is it possible that the gospel calls us not only to not take offense—but also to try to understand why the Qur'an treats the Resurrection in this apparently cavalier way?

The Texts
THE BIBLE
Mark 15:25–39; 16:1–6

It was nine o'clock in the morning when they crucified him. The inscription of the charge against him read, "The King of the Jews." And with him they crucified two bandits, one on his right and one on his left. Those who passed by derided him, shaking their heads and saying, "Aha! You who would destroy the temple and build it in three days, save yourself, and come down from the cross!" In the same way the chief priests, along with the scribes, were also mocking him among themselves and saying, "He saved others; he cannot save himself. Let the Messiah, the King of Israel, come down from the cross now, so that we may see and believe." Those who were crucified with him also taunted him.

When it was noon, darkness came over the whole land until three in the afternoon. At three o'clock Jesus cried out with a loud voice, "Eloi, Eloi, lema sabachthani?" which means, "My God, my God, why have you forsaken me?" When some of the bystanders heard it, they said, "Listen, he is calling for Elijah." And someone ran, filled a sponge with sour wine, put it on a stick, and gave it to him to drink, saying, "Wait, let us see whether Elijah will come to take him down." Then Jesus gave a loud cry and breathed his last. And the curtain of the temple was torn in two, from top to bottom. Now when the centurion, who stood facing him, saw that in this way he breathed his last, he said, "Truly this man was God's Son!"...

When the sabbath was over, Mary Magdalene, and Mary the mother of James, and Salome bought spices, so that they might go and anoint him. And very early on the first day of the week, when the sun had risen, they went to the tomb. They had been saying to one another, "Who will roll away the stone for us from the entrance to the tomb?" When they looked up, they saw that the stone, which was very large, had already been rolled back. As they entered the tomb, they saw a young man, dressed in a white robe, sitting on the right side; and they were alarmed. But he said to them, "Do not be alarmed; you are looking for Jesus of Nazareth, who was crucified. He has been raised; he is not here. Look, there is the place they laid him.

THE QUR'AN
sura nisa' "Women" 4:155–159

[4:155]Here are the reasons why the People of the Book, or the Jews, have incurred God's anger: Because they broke their Covenant, and because they did not believe God's signs and warnings, and because they killed the prophets against all justice, and because they boasted, "Our hearts have sealed up all truth inside them."— No, not at all! It is God who has sealed up their hearts for their defiant self-sufficiency. Only a very few of them are open to God. [4:156]And more reasons still: because they rejected faith, and because they slandered Mary, the mother of 'Isa, claiming that she was a fornicator. [4:157]And because they said in their pride, "Look! We have killed 'Isa, son of Mary and Messenger of God!" Yet they did not in fact kill him—nor did they crucify him. They only seemed to do so. [Other possible translation: "He only appeared to be crucified."] Those who dispute about what happened are truly in doubt about it. They have no sound knowledge and merely follow their own opinion. What is sure is that the Jews did not kill him. [4:158]Sure also is this—that God raised him up to himself. God is beyond all comparison for power, beyond all comparison for wisdom. [4:159]There is no member of the People of the Book who will not believe in 'Isa before 'Isa's death on the Last Day. [Other possible translation: "There is no member of the People of the Book who will not before his own death be duty bound to believe in 'Isa."] For on the Last Day he will witness in his favor or against it.

GUIDED DISCUSSION QUESTIONS
1. *Do the differences among the four Gospel accounts of the Crucifixion cast doubt on the Crucifixion's truth?*
This question sounds absurd to our Christian ears. We all accept the many differences in the styles and in the details with

which the four Gospel writers tell the story of Jesus' death, without thinking for a moment that the variety puts the truth of the story in doubt. Yet many Muslims advance just such an objection. They are used to a scripture coming from one source alone, from God himself, a source from which no Muslim would ever dream that there could a diversity of view on what is obviously such an important issue.

What would you say to help your Muslim friends understand your willingness to accept as true four different versions of the Crucifixion story?

Note that this is a very different challenge from trying to persuade them of that truth. Can you put in your own words the difference between "helping to understand" and "persuading"?

2. Should we Christians take offense at a grammatical ambiguity?
The only time the Qur'an makes any sort of reference to the Crucifixion is in *sura* 4:157. Yet the key part of this phrase, the part in the middle that ought to explain what did actually happen on Calvary, turns out to be impenetrable grammatically. Literally the key phrase says: "It—or he—was made to appear to them so." If we take "he" as the subject, then we end up with something like "He only appeared to be crucified." Some Muslim interpreters expand on this version to say that at the last moment a look-alike was put up on the cross in Jesus' place while Jesus was spirited away safe and sound. But that interpretation is felt by the majority of Muslims to do little honor to Jesus as a prophet. These Muslim interpreters argue that Jesus' willingness to suffer must be respected. Only God could and did intervene in such an impasse, rescuing Jesus alive and causing a phantom to appear in his place. Such interpreters prefer the translation, "They only seemed to crucify him" or "It only seemed to them that they had crucified him."

Now that you see something of the struggle Muslims them-selves have had with the ambiguous Qur'anic phrase in *sura* 4:157, are you more inclined to admit the positive aspects of the Muslim point of view?

3. *Is the Qur'an's ambiguity about what happened to Jesus on Calvary and afterward a sign of disrespect for Jesus?*
In the previous question we looked at the ambiguity of the Qur'an's language in regard to the Crucifixion. But the Qur'an is every bit as ambiguous about subsequent events. Yes, the Qur'an does say clearly, "God raised him up to himself." But if Jesus did not die on the cross, as the Qur'an so vigorously insists, then does this statement mean that Jesus was taken up alive, like Elijah? The next line, unfortunately, does not clarify matters. The "death" referred to in line 4:159 might refer to that of any Jewish person who at the last moment of life will finally have to confess that Jesus was a prophet of God. But that inter-pretation would seem to make Jesus' role at the Last Day super-fluous if all who deny his prophethood repent of their ways before death. Most Muslims prefer a translation that speaks of Jesus' own death. In this scenario, Jesus, having been taken up alive to heaven, will remain alive until the Last Day, at which time he along with all others alive at that moment will die. Jesus will be resurrected along with all other mortals, but, because of his special status as prophet, he will be given the role of "wit-ness" for and against the Jews. Muslim belief has subsequently interpreted his role more broadly as that of universal witness for and against all the dead. Indeed, Jesus' assumption of the role of chief witness is considered by most Muslims to be a sign that the Day of Judgment has arrived.

Keeping in mind the Qur'an's great interest in vindicating Jesus' career as a prophet uniquely born of a virgin, why might the Qur'an actually want to treat the events of the Crucifixion and Resurrection vaguely, with ambiguity? In any case, do you think that the Qur'an means disrespect to Jesus by apparently refusing to spell out with absolute clarity Jesus' status at the Crucifixion and afterward?

4. Does the statement in 4:158–"Sure also is this–that God raised him up to himself"–have the same meaning to Christians as it does to Muslims?

The statement in question seems to echo various lines from the New Testament. For example, Peter says to the crowd gathered around the eleven and the other disciples at Pentecost, "You that are Israelites...this man...you crucified and killed...God raised him up, having freed him from death, because it was impossible for him to be held in its power" (Acts 2:22–24). Here, as in the Qur'an, the assertion is made that the Jews were not able to kill Jesus after all and that he was raised up to God. Christians and Muslims seem to be saying the same thing!

But are they? How great are the similarities between the Qur'an and Acts on this point? How great are the differences?

5. Does the statement in sura 4:159–"And on the Last Day he will witness for or against them"–mean the same thing to Christians as it does to Muslims?

This phrase, like the phrase from 4:158 just discussed, seems to echo language from the New Testament. Matthew 25:32 says, for example, that "...he will separate people one from another as a shepherd separates the sheep from the goats...." Here again Christians and Muslims seem to be saying the same thing.

But are they? Do you think "separating" and "witnessing" mean the same thing? (You may want to come back to this question after you've tackled the chapter on Judgment.)

CHAPTER TEN

WHAT DO WE EACH BELIEVE ABOUT JESUS' RELATION TO GOD?

Introduction

The differences between Jesus and 'Isa will arouse a variety of reactions in us Christians, some of them negative: reactions such as impatience, frustration, perhaps even offense. But the better we understand the Qur'an's point of view, the greater the possibility that more positive reactions will ensue: reactions such as puzzlement, curiosity, perhaps even fascination.

The more positive responses don't mean we're on a slippery slope to a disastrous end such as apostasy. They mean that we've been able to make the imaginative leap into our Muslim brother's or sister's shoes. We've begun to see Jesus through his or her eyes. The benefit for us of doing so is that, once we're wearing our own shoes again, we can see "our" Jesus with fresh vision. He will stand out more clearly.

Perhaps the more positive responses will begin to emerge here at the end of our chapters on Jesus. We're well aware now that when we speak of Jesus and 'Isa, we are talking about beings who are intimately related and at the same time profoundly different. We are no longer shocked at the paradoxical connection between them. What we seek to know now is what to make of the paradox. Does the paradox have constructive value for our interfaith understanding?

We can begin to answer this question by meditating on the two passages that follow. At first glance, these passages will probably seem more different than they are alike. The passage from John's Gospel comes at the end of chapter 12. This passage covers the events of the critical week preceding the Passover and the Last Supper. Jesus is aware of the fear and hatred he has aroused among the Jewish authorities. He predicts his imminent death, and for a moment he seems to waver in his mission ("Now my soul is troubled..." 12:27), but quickly he regains his steadiness. Then he hides from his persecutors. From that hidden place Jesus speaks about his relation to God for the benefit of his disciples in the first passage below.

The parallel passage from the Qur'an takes place on Judgment Day—but also in a kind of eternal present (that is, as if seen through God's perspective on time). 'Isa, just as every other mortal must eventually do, is laying bare the truth of his life on earth directly to God. He testifies to his strict adherence to his prophetic mandate and denies the imputation that he ever set himself up as a god within a kind of divine triad including his mother Mary and God himself as third party.

The place, the time, the occasion and the audience for Jesus' and 'Isa's assertions couldn't look more different. So what can the two passages have in common? Actually, quite a lot! Assessing those similarities will help us refine our understanding of where the real differences occur.

The Texts
THE BIBLE
John 12:44–50

Then Jesus cried aloud: "Whoever believes in me believes not in me but in him who sent me. And whoever sees me sees him who sent me. I have come as light into the world, so that everyone who believes in me should not remain in the darkness. I do not judge anyone who hears my words and does not keep them, for I came not to judge the world, but to save the world. The one who rejects me and does not receive my word has a judge; on the last day the word that I have spoken will serve as judge, for I have not spoken on my own, but the Father who sent me has himself given me a commandment about what to say and what to speak. And I know that his commandment is eternal life. What I speak, therefore, I speak just as the Father has told me."

THE QUR'AN
sura al-ma'idah "The Spread Table" 5:116–120

5:116And see! God will say on that Last Day, "O 'Isa, son of Mary, did you ever say to humankind, 'Take me and my mother as two gods along with God as a third?' 'Isa will reply, "Praise be to you! The last thing I would say is what I would have no business saying. Even if I had said such a thing, you would have known it. You know well what is in my soul, but I do not know what is in yours. For you alone know all those things that are hidden. 5:117I never said anything to people except as you commanded me. For example—'Worship God, your Cherisher and Sustainer.' And I was a witness over them during the time I lived among them. Then when you took me to yourself, you were the watcher. For you are a witness over all things. 5:118So if you punish them, they are your servants. If you forgive them, you are beyond all measure of power, beyond all measure of wisdom."

5:119Then God will say: "This is the Day when the truthful ones will profit from their truthfulness. To them belong the gardens with cool rivers flowing beneath where they will live eternally—God delighting in them, and they in God." 5:120To God belong the kingdoms of heaven and earth and all that is in them. For God holds mastery over all things.

GUIDED DISCUSSION QUESTIONS

1. *Do Jesus and 'Isa have a similar relation to God?*
Note that the Jesus of the Gospel proclaims, "I speak just as the Father has told me" (John 12:50). "Their" 'Isa asserts, "I never said anything to people except as you commanded me."

Do these proclamations reveal that there is something similar in Jesus and 'Isa's relation to God? What might that similarity be?

2. *Do Jesus and 'Isa proclaim a similar message?*
To back up his assertion that he "never said anything to people except as you commanded me," 'Isa gives the following example: "Worship God, your Cherisher and Sustainer." "Worship" in this context means total devotion to God's will, not one's own.

It's true that Jesus doesn't say anything quite like that in the passage from John. But there would seem to be other places in the Gospels where Jesus does say something similar (see Jesus' commandments in Mark 12:31; see also Matthew 22:37 and Luke 10:27).

What do you think? How similar are 'Isa's and Jesus' messages?

3. *Do Jesus and 'Isa respond to tests to their fidelity in a similar way?*
As indicated in the introduction to this chapter, Jesus is faced with a test of his fidelity to his mission in John 12. As for 'Isa, he finds himself at Judgment Day, the moment for absolute truth-telling. There, according to the Qur'an, all our tricks, subterfuges and self-justifications will be put in plain view before God and all the angels and prophets. Similarly, all our acts of charity and devotion to God will be laid bare as well. Heaven or hell await us based on the outcome of our self-display. (See chapter sixteen for more about Judgment.)

Given the circumstances, how does 'Isa handle the moment of truth? Does Jesus handle his moment of truth similarly? (Don't be misled by the word "he cried aloud" in John 12:44. "Cried aloud" doesn't mean that Jesus spoke in pain or anguish. Determine the phrase's exact meaning by assessing the three other places where it is used in John 1:15; 7:28, 37.)

4. Does 'Isa's declaration that he is not a god like God carve an unbridgeable gulf between himself and Jesus?
Focusing on 'Isa's and Jesus' possible similarities doesn't, of course, take away from their fundamental difference (the difference between 'Isa respected as prophet and Jesus worshiped as God's Son). The question is not whether 'Isa and Jesus are different at all but whether this difference is absolute, without any linking or kinship. What makes our assessment more complicated is the perhaps surprising fact that we Christians are as adamantly opposed to the imputation 'Isa in *al-ma'idah* refutes about himself at Judgment Day as Muslims are. Christianity, like Islam, has always fought vigorously against tritheism—the belief that the Trinity is a triad of three *different* gods. Christianity, like Islam, has fought vigorously also against what might be called Mariolatry: the worship of Mary as a goddess, a kind of fourth member of a Christian pantheon—or even a third member, as the Qur'an pictures it. So despite the fact Muslims and Christians differ fundamentally about 'Isa's and Jesus' natures or identities, we are nevertheless united in opposition to some of the same false beliefs about 'Isa and Jesus.

In the light of these facts, facts both about 'Isa's and Jesus' similarities and about their great difference, how deep would you say the gulf is between 'Isa the prophet and Jesus the Son of God? In your view, is it unbridgeable?

CHAPTER ELEVEN

WHAT DO WE EACH BELIEVE ABOUT THE HOLY SPIRIT?

Introduction

The Holy Spirit is another topic where caution and charity are needed. As with Jesus and 'Isa, the Spirit is a topic that Christians and Muslims can easily find themselves arguing about, creating more heat than light. The reason for this is, again, that each religion jealously guards its own understanding of the topic. They do so because the topic in question goes to the heart of what is unique about each religion—and what must be accepted as true against all opposing views.

The fact that Christians and Muslims say very similar things about the Spirit doesn't ease the tension. The similarities merely serve to make the differences stand out with greater force.

For both Christians and Muslims, the Spirit is pictured as a breath of God, active at Adam's creation and at Jesus' as well. Both Christians and Muslims believe fervently in the Virgin Birth through the Spirit. Both see Jesus and 'Isa strengthened by the Spirit throughout their lives and even made one with it.

But while, according to the Qur'an, human beings are creatures uniquely empowered by God's *ruh* or spirit, this *ruh* is no more than a power or attribute of God. As a result, the Qur'anic *ruh* exerts a less transforming effect on us than does the Holy Spirit. Not that the power of the Qur'anic *ruh* is negligible. Far from it! This *ruh* endows us with free will so that we might know and praise God. For according to the Qur'an it is through such knowledge and praise that we fulfill our creaturely natures as human beings. Our earthly life is the testing ground for the exercise of the gift of free will. Heaven—or hell—marks the degree to which we use the gift of God's *ruh*. Yet for all of its power and importance, the Qur'anic *ruh* does not usher us into the very life of God. The Qur'anic *ruh* is not the Spirit acting to bring us into unity with Jesus and through Jesus into unity with the Father.

The difference between the Qur'anic *ruh* and our Christian Holy Spirit mirrors the difference between 'Isa and Jesus discussed in previous chapters. 'Isa, like Adam, is a creature conceived through the *ruh*. The *ruh* is the means of 'Isa's and Adam's creation, but the *ruh* is not itself their creator. Accordingly, 'Isa's and Adam's conceptions testify, not to the *ruh*, but to God, who, as the Qur'an repeats frequently, "only has to say 'Let it be' and it exists." The *ruh* is never identified or made equal with God, any more than 'Isa is.

Another conflicting understanding of the Spirit arises in the way the New Testament and the Qur'an talk about the Paraclete. The conflict turns on what seems to be a mere difference in the way the word *Paraclete* is spelled. Yet underlying the apparently trivial basis of the conflict is a deep difference about what constitutes each religion's ultimate authority: God's sending of the Spirit at Pentecost versus God's sending of the revelation to Muhammad. The conflict in question seems to pit one religion's understanding of that authority against the other's.

The Texts
THE BIBLE
John 14:15–17; 20:19–23

"If you love me, you will keep my commandments. And I will ask the Father, and he will give you another Advocate, to be with you for ever. This is the Spirit of truth, whom the world cannot receive, because it neither sees him nor knows him. You know him, because he abides with you, and he will be in you...."

When it was evening on that day, the first day of the week, and the doors of the house where the disciples had met were locked for fear of the Jews, Jesus came and stood among them and said, "Peace be with you." After he said this, he showed them his hands and his side. Then the disciples rejoiced when they saw the Lord. Jesus said to them again, "Peace be with you. As the Father has sent me, so I send you." When he had said this, he breathed on them and said to them, "Receive the Holy Spirit. If you forgive the sins of any, they are forgiven them; if you retain the sins of any, they are retained."

THE QUR'AN
sura al-baqarah "The Heifer" 2:87; 3:49

2:87We gave Moses the Book of the Torah and caused Messengers to follow in succession after him. And we gave 'Isa the Son of Mary clear Signs and strengthened him by the Holy Spirit....

3:49And God will appoint 'Isa a Messenger to the Children of Israel. "For see," 'Isa will say, "I have come to you with a Sign from your Cherisher and Sustainer. I create for you from clay something in the form of a bird. I breathe into it and it becomes a real bird by God's will. And I heal those blind from birth as well as lepers, and I bring the dead to life by God's will."

sura al-saff "Battle Array" 61:6

61:6Remember when 'Isa son of Mary said, "I am indeed a Messenger of God sent to you to confirm the Torah which came before my time and the Good News of a Messenger to come after me whose name shall be Ahmad [i.e., 'the most praised one']." But when the prophet came among them with clear signs, they said, "This is clear witchcraft!"

GUIDED DISCUSSION QUESTIONS

1. *Do Jesus and 'Isa breathe the same Spirit?*
Think about the parallels between Jesus' breathing the Spirit on the disciples in John 20:21–23 and 'Isa's breathing the Spirit into the clay bird in *sura al-baqarah* 3:49.

In what way do the actions of breathing by Jesus and 'Isa have a similar effect? In what way are the disciples in their locked room a little bit like birds of clay? How are the effects at the same time vastly different?

2. *Why isn't breathing a clay bird into life a "Christian" miracle?*
Think about the fact that the miracle of breathing the clay bird into life is attributed not only to 'Isa but to Jesus as well in the apocryphal gospel of Thomas, as well as in other apocryphal gospels.

Why do you suppose this miracle never made it into our canonical Gospels? Is there something about this miracle that violates our Christian image of Jesus' power or our image of the way he would have been likely to use it? Clearly, the miracle, far from violating Muslims' image of 'Isa's power, actually confirms the fact that 'Isa is indeed a "sign" of God. Why do you suppose that a miracle which validates 'Isa apparently does not or cannot do the same for Jesus?

3. Does Jesus prophesy the coming of Muhammad?

In the Qur'an, 'Isa says to the Jews, "I am indeed a Messenger of God sent to you to confirm the Torah which came before my time and the Good News of a Messenger to come after me whose name shall be Ahmad [i.e., 'the most praised one']." The Qur'anic line seems to echo a line like this one from John's Gospel: "I will ask the Father, and he will give you another Advocate, who will be with you forever. This is the Spirit of truth..." (14:16–17). So while Jesus in John's Gospel gives the good news of the coming of the Advocate or Spirit of truth, 'Isa in the Qur'an promises the coming of a Messenger called Ahmad. But are Ahmad and the Paraclete the same?

Well, yes...and no! First off, "Ahmad" is an alternate form of the name Muhammad. (Muhammad means "the praised one." Ahmad means "the most praised one.") Muslims see Muhammad beautifully fulfilling the role of Comforter and Spirit of truth. Some Muslim scholars make an additional claim. They say that the Greek word *perikletos* translated in New Testament texts as "Advocate" (and anglicized as "Paraclete") is an error and that the text really ought to read *periklutos*, which means "greatly celebrated, greatly praised," i.e., Ahmad. This conflict of interpretation may seem based on trivialities, especially the one based on the difference of one vowel in *perikletos* versus *periklutos*. Yet the consequences of the conflict, as remarked above, are anything but trivial. Obviously neither Muslims nor Christians are prepared to budge an inch from their very different readings of *perikletos* and *periklutos*.

Rather than enter into a futile dispute, what if we Christians tried to understand what is being said in the Qur'anic version?

It is in the spirit of mutual understanding that the following questions are asked: How is the power of prophecy given 'Isa in the Qur'anic account of the Paraclete like and unlike the power of prophecy given Jesus in the Gospel of John? In what way did the subsequent coming of Muhammad have an effect on the world in some ways similar to the effect of the coming of the Holy Spirit at Pentecost?

Such questions should not lead to our blurring the two events—to do so would be a betrayal not only of our own beliefs as Christians but also of Muslims' beliefs as well. The questions are useful as ways of appreciating what the Qur'an is saying here about the link between 'Isa, Muhammad and God's *ruh*—and of appreciating precisely how our Christian understanding of the link between Jesus and the Holy Spirit is different.

CHAPTER TWELVE

WHAT DO WE EACH BELIEVE ABOUT PRAYER?

Introduction

Our basic Christian prayer, the Our Father, and the basic prayer of Muslims, *sura al-fatihah* "The Opening," have much in common.

What they have in common is, first, that both are prayers given to us by God as models for our own prayers. Both of them are short and approximately of the same length. Both begin by calling upon and praising God. Both move quickly from praise to petition. And the petitions themselves move from positive to negative: from asking for help and guidance to seeking protection against going astray.

Another common feature is that the Our Father and *sura al-fatihah* are eminently communal prayers which take their place at the center of each religion's liturgies. Catholic Christians recite the Our Father at Sunday and daily Masses, during the Liturgy of the Hours and during the rosary. Muslims hear and respond to *sura al-fatihah* a total of seventeen times a day each day of the week during *salat*, the five prescribed daily public prayers.

A third common feature has to do with the way both prayers challenge hypocrisy and idolatry. This feature is seen in their origins. *Sura al-fatihah* challenged pagan prayer to multiple or fictitious gods. The Lord's Prayer challenged the dominant prayer forms of Palestinian culture: the wordiness of the Pharisees' prayers and the idolatry of the Romans' prayers to their deified emperors.

The differences between the prayers—for of course there are some—stem largely from differences between the New Testament and the Qur'an as scriptures.

The Our Father comes to us in two quite different versions, that of Luke (probably the earliest version) and that of Matthew. Or actually in three, if we include the doxology ("For thine is the Kingdom…"), which doesn't occur in the New Testament at all but in the second-century *Didache*. These two (or three) versions show how Jesus' words were shaped by Luke's and Matthew's faith communities to reflect those communities' different understandings of the Christ event. By contrast, *sura al-fatihah*—like all of the Qur'an—is believed to be the direct speech of God sent down to Muhammad. So there can be no such thing as a "version" of *sura al-fatihah*. More than that, while the Our Father occurs within Luke's and Matthew's accounts of Jesus' teachings on prayer, *sura al-fatihah* is quite literally the gateway or "opening" to the whole Qur'an. As the first of the Qur'an's 114 suras, it prays that God "guide us on the straight path.…" The rest of the Qur'an is that very guidance. Muslims call attention to *sura al-fatihah*'s importance as portal to the Qur'anic edifice by beautifully illuminating it with calligraphic designs in most editions of the Qur'an.

The Texts

THE BIBLE

Luke 11:1-4

He was praying in a certain place, and after he had finished, one of his disciples said to him, "Lord, teach us to pray, as John taught his disciples." He said to them, "When you pray, say:

Father, hallowed be your name

Your kingdom come.

Give us each day our daily bread.

And forgive us our sins,

for we ourselves forgive everyone indebted to us.

And do not bring us to the time of trial."

Matthew 6:9-13

Pray then in this way:

Our Father in heaven,

hallowed be your name.

Your kingdom come.

Your will be done,

on earth as it is in heaven.

Give us this day our daily bread.

And forgive us our debts,

as we also have forgiven

our debtors.

And do not bring us to the time of trial,

but rescue us from the evil one."

THE QUR'AN

sura al-fatihah "The Opening" 1:1-7

1:1In the name of God, the most beneficent, the most merciful.

1:2Praise belongs to God, the Cherisher and Sustainer of all the worlds,

1:3The most beneficent, the most merciful,

1:4The master of the Day of Judgment.

1:5It is you we worship, it is you we ask for help.
1:6Guide us on the straight path,
1:7The path of those to whom you have given your favor,
  not those upon whom there is wrath or who have gone astray.

GUIDED DISCUSSION QUESTIONS

1. *Why are Muslims uneasy with the phrase "Our Father who art in heaven..."?*
Even though there are no statements in the Our Father that call attention to the major sources of disagreement between Christians and Muslims—no statements about Christ as Son of God or about God as a Trinity, for example—there are still wordings that disconcert many Muslims. Take the innocent sounding "our" in "our Father." Muslims contrast the possessive "our" with the corresponding phrase *from sura al-fatihāh*, "the Cherisher and Sustainer of all the worlds...."

Why do you think the use of "our" makes Muslims uneasy? What do we appear to be saying about God that would make them uneasy? What could we say to correct their misunderstanding?

Muslims are also uneasy about calling God "Father." The word "father" seems to bring God down to our level. But they're uneasy also at describing God as "who art in heaven"—which seems to put God too far away. What does Muslims' uneasiness with what they regard as extreme ways of referring to God tell us about their own understanding of who God is? What could we say that might help them see that our understanding is not so different from theirs?

2. *Why are Muslims uneasy with the use of certain verbs in the Our Father?*
"Hallowed be your name. Your kingdom come. Your will be done...." These verb forms expressing wishes sound to

Muslims as if we are praying *for* God rather than *to* him. Muslims contrast the apparent uncertainty about whether God *will* in fact be praised ("hallowed") or whether his kingdom *will* come or with whether his will *will* be done with the definiteness of *sura al-fatihah's* "Praise belongs to God...."

What different ideas about God's relation to time and history are suggested by Muslims' uneasiness?

3. In the Our Father, are humans setting themselves up as examples for God to follow?
That's the conclusion Muslims draw from Matthew's "And forgive us our debts, as [i.e., to the extent that] we also have forgiven our debtors." Muslims would be happier with Luke's "And forgive us our sins, for we ourselves forgive everyone indebted to us...." Muslims would compare Luke's version favorably with *sura an-nur* 24:22:

> Let not those of you who are blessed with favor and wealth resolve by oath not to help their relatives, those who are destitute, and those who have left everything behind in God's cause. But instead let them forgive and overlook all offenses. Don't you wish God to forgive you? For God himself is all-forgiving, most merciful.

How would you explain to Muslims why we commonly say Matthew's version (with its special understanding of forgiveness) and not Luke's?

4. Is sura al-fatihah *a prayer that we Christians can pray?*
Although Muslims have reservations such as the ones just listed about praying the Our Father, they see no reason why we Christians can't use *sura al-fatihah* in our own prayer. They say that Islam came to confirm what Muslims regard as the core teachings of all previous scriptures, especially those of Judaism

and Christianity, and that therefore Islam's prayers are the only truly universal ones.

Weighing the words of *sura al-fatihah* carefully, would you agree with this assessment? Is there something in *sura al-fatihah* you could *not* pray? Why not?

CHAPTER THIRTEEN

WHAT DO WE EACH BELIEVE ABOUT HUMAN BLESSEDNESS?

Introduction

What Christians believe about human blessedness seems clear enough. The Beatitudes say it all, don't they?

Well, yes and no. The Beatitudes do indeed list certain desirable human behaviors or states in the "Blessed be" or "Blessed are" form. The complicating factors are that the Beatitudes exist in two versions, Luke's and Matthew's, and that these two versions have different emphases. Luke's Beatitudes commend those who suffer greatly from social exclusion and persecution, while Matthew's Beatitudes honor more inward states of humility and holiness. (Compare Luke's "Blessed are the poor" with Matthew's "Blessed are the poor in spirit.") These differences largely reflect the fact that Luke and Matthew shaped their material for different communities. Luke's community—to cite just one difference—probably contained more poor people than Matthew's.

Despite this and other differences, both Luke's and Matthew's communities were alike in sharing the memory of persecution by both the Jewish authorities and the Romans. But their communities shared something more fundamental still: a belief that human blessedness arises in response to Jesus' announcement of the coming "kingdom of Heaven" in Matthew's phrase and "kingdom of God" in Luke's. Human blessedness follows from belief in a future transformation of the world whose initial steps have already been taken in the life and ministry of Jesus Christ.

Looking at the passage from *sura al-furqan* in the following section that in both style and content resembles the Beatitudes, we discover some interesting contrasts. One of them is that here is no question of "versions." The revelation of *al-furqan* came through only one person, Muhammad, and to only one community, the *umma* of Mecca. Another is that while we know that the Meccan community was persecuted, the degree of that persecution was much less severe than in Matthew's and especially in Luke's communities. But the overriding difference between the Christian and what we might call the Qur'anic Beatitudes is in orientation to the present moment. The Qur'an links human blessedness, not to a future fulfillment, but to creation viewed as a continuous process, active at each instant. For Islam, the present moment opens directly into the eternity of God's creating presence. For Christians, by contrast, the present moment looks forward to the coming of Christ, who will appear at the end of time to inaugurate "new heavens and a new earth, where righteousness is at home" (2 Peter 3:13).

The consequence of this difference for human blessedness is that in *sura-furqan* (and in the Qur'an generally) blessedness is more practical, more within actual human reach. Blessedness falls within the range of what human beings can achieve here and now, within a specific existing community. In the Christian Beatitudes, human blessedness follows either from a revolutionary transformation of human society, in Luke's version, or from a revolutionary transformation of the human heart, in Matthew's. These two transformations aren't mutually exclusive, of course. One depends on the other. But neither—nor both together—can happen in the normal course of events. Their fulfillment awaits God's coming. The blessed wait in hope.

The Texts
THE BIBLE
Matthew 5:2–11

Then he began to speak, and taught them, saying:

"Blessed are the poor in spirit, for theirs is the kingdom of heaven.

"Blessed are those who mourn, for they will be comforted.

"Blessed are the meek, for they will inherit the earth.

"Blessed are those who hunger and thirst for righteousness, for they will be filled.

"Blessed are the merciful, for they will receive mercy.

"Blessed are the pure in heart, for they will see God.

"Blessed are the peacemakers, for they will be called children of God.

"Blessed are those who are persecuted for righteousness' sake, for theirs is the kingdom of heaven.

"Blessed are you when people revile you and persecute you and utter all kinds of evil against you falsely on my account."

Luke 6:20–25

Then he looked up at his disciples and said:

"Blessed are you who are poor,
> for yours is the kingdom of God.

"Blessed are you who are hungry now,
> for you will be filled.

"Blessed are you who weep now,
> for you will laugh.

"Blessed are you when people hate you, and when they exclude you, revile you, and defame you on account of the Son of Man. Rejoice on that day and leap for joy, for surely your reward is great in heaven; for that is what their ancestors did to the prophets.

"But woe to you who are rich,
  for you have received your consolation.
"Woe to you who are full now,
  for you will be hungry.
"Woe to you who are laughing now,
  for you will mourn and weep."

THE QUR'AN
sura al-furqan "The Criterion" 25:61–76

25:61Blessed be God, who placed those ornaments—the constellations—in the heavens. And within the constellations he placed a candle—the sun—and a moon reflecting the sun's light. 25:62And God is he who created the night and the day and then caused them to follow each other for the benefit of whoever yearns to admonish himself or herself and to be grateful to him.

25:63For the servants of the Merciful One are those who walk humbly on the earth, and when the violent and impatient address them, they calmly say, "Salaam, peace."

25:64Those are the ones who pass the night praising their Cherisher and Sustainer, bowing down low and standing up straight again.

25:65Those are the ones who exclaim, "O our Cherisher and Sustainer, turn away from us the torment of hell. For its torment is never-ending. 25:66Hell is an evil place to stay in, whether for a short time or long."

25:67Those are the ones who when they spend their substance are neither extravagant nor stingy but keep a firm balance between extremes.

25:68Those are the ones who do not call out to any other god but God, nor do they take life except for just cause, nor do they fornicate. Anyone who does such things meets with punishment.

25:69And the punishment will be doubled on the Last Day, and the perpetrator will dwell in the deepest disgrace 25:70unless he repents and believes and does righteous deeds. For then God will exchange his evil for good. God is all-forgiving, all-merciful. 25:71For the one who repents and does righteous deeds, truly has he turned back to God in the deepest turning.

25:72Blessed also are they who neither swear falsely nor associate themselves with falsehood in any way. And if they should happen on vain talk, they pass on by with gracious avoidance.

25:73Those are the ones who, when admonished by signs from their Cherisher and Sustainer, do not yawn at those signs as if they themselves were deaf and blind.

25:74Those are the ones who say, "Our Cherisher and Sustainer, give us spouses and children to 'cool our eye'—to delight and comfort us. And give us the wisdom to be leaders of the God-conscious among us.

25:75Those are the ones who will receive a place in the Seventh Heaven for their long suffering patience. And they shall meet there a word of life, fullness of being, salaam... 25:76dwelling in that Heaven, a beautiful place to stay in, whether for a short time or long.

25:77Say this, Muhammad, to the others: "My Cherisher and Sustainer will not be concerned for you unless you call out to him. But now you have rejected him. Your punishment will not be long in coming."

GUIDED DISCUSSION QUESTIONS

1. *What can we learn from the rising of the sun?*

In verse 62 of *al-furqan* we read that "God...created the night and the day and then caused them to follow each other for the benefit of those who yearn to admonish him or herself and to be grateful to him."

What is the Qur'an's logic here? Why should those particular divine actions cause us to admonish ourselves and be grateful to God? Admonish ourselves for what? Be grateful to God for what? Perhaps look back at chapter three to recall the way creation is presented in the Qur'an.

2. Can Christians connect to the Qur'an's linking of creation with self-admonishment?
Consider what Saint Paul says in Romans 1:18–20: "For the wrath of God is revealed from heaven against all ungodliness and wickedness of those who by their wickedness suppress the truth. For what can be known about God is plain to them, because God has shown it to them. Ever since the creation of the world his eternal power and divine nature, invisible though they are, have been understood and seen through the things he has made. So they are without excuse."

Can you find connections between what Saint Paul says in Romans 1:18–20 and verse 61 of *al-furqan*? Have you yourself ever sensed God's "eternal power and divine nature...through the things that he has made"? Has your sensing of God's "eternal power" stimulated you to self-admonishment and gratitude?

3. What are the different expectations for Christian and Qur'anic blessedness?
One way to check these differences is to compare passages that evoke similar challenges to the blessed person. For example, verse 63 of *al-furqan* sets out a certain standard for blessed behavior when facing persecutors: ("...when the violent and impatient address them, they calmly say, 'Salaam, peace'"). Compare that prescribed behavior with the behavior commended in Matthew 5:11 ("Blessed are you when people revile you..."). How would you describe the difference in what is expected of the blessed person in this instance?

Another way is to look at the difference in the overall tone of behavior urged upon the blessed. We've just seen how the Qur'an urges the blessed to respond "calmly" to insult. Note also in verse 67 of *al-furqan* the emphasis is on keeping a "firm balance between extremes." What tone of behavior is commended in the Christian Beatitudes?

Still another way is to look at the content of the blessed life, especially the references to killing and fornicating in verse 68 of *al-furqan*, swearing falsely in verse 72, enjoying one's family in verse 74.

Nothing like this is found in the Christian Beatitudes. Why not? What content is found instead? How would you explain the difference in content?

4. Can Christians help Muslims understand why human blessedness includes "turning the other cheek"?

Luke's and Matthew's Beatitudes stand at the beginning of long sections collecting many of Jesus' most famous—and most difficult—teachings. (Luke's section is often called "The Sermon on the Plain"; Matthew's, "The Sermon on the Mount.") Among Jesus' teachings is one Muslims find particularly difficult to understand. This is the one about "turning the other cheek" as found in both Gospels, in Matthew 5:39 and Luke 6:29.

Can you see why Muslims, given their own expectations for human blessedness, tend to find Jesus' commandment to "turn the other cheek" unfathomable, nonsensical and even perverse (since it seems to invite victimization)? How would you explain to them that "turning the other check" is both a powerful assertion of Christian dignity and a creative act of peacemaking? (Remember that many Christians also have trouble with this commandment and avoid talking about it.)

CHAPTER FOURTEEN

WHAT DO WE EACH BELIEVE ABOUT THE GREATER JIHAD?

Introduction

According to one of the *hadith,* or authenticated reports of the Prophet Muhammad's sayings—and a source of guidance for Muslims second only to the Qur'an—Muhammad returned from a decisive battle with his Meccan enemies and said, "You have returned from the lesser Jihad to the greater." When asked what he meant by "greater," he replied, "It is the Jihad against your passionate souls."

This comment must have come as a shock to the assembled troops and their families, because the battle in question was won over great odds and had given a tremendous boost to the young and beleaguered Muslim community. Right at the height of their celebration, Muhammad announces that victory in a just cause is good, but a lesser good! Something else is more important. What is it?

We start by observing that the Arabic word *Jihad* means "striving for any good end." As used in the Qur'an and by Muhammad in the speech above, Jihad means striving to obey God's call that we praise him and serve his creation. Jihad has an inward and outward direction. The inward one is most important. Without secure focus on the goal of all striving on Islam or self-yielding to God and to him alone, Jihad becomes the plaything of one's passions. Once that inner focus is firm, then Jihad may be safely directed outward, toward upholding and, if necessary—and only then if one is able, and always under strict conditions—toward defending the community.

Although the word Jihad isn't actually used very much in the Qur'an, its basic meaning informs just about every appeal the Qur'an makes. That's because, according to the Qur'an, we human beings come into the world fully equipped with God's favor or grace. The issue for us is, are we going to respond to this favor or not? The response requires Jihad or striving, yes. But the demand is not beyond our strength. What is required is that we rouse ourselves from sluggishness and forgetfulness so that we can attend to the one thing necessary: God's unceasing effort to remind us that the only real good in life comes to us through worship of him. All other objects of striving—of Jihad—are not only illusory. They are utterly destructive.

The story of Joseph and his brothers, as the Qur'an tells it, gives concrete meaning to the concept of the Greater Jihad. True, the word *Jihad* is not used in what the Qur'an calls "this most beautiful of all stories." But Joseph's and his father Jacob's patience and trust in God in the face of enmity and betrayal are powerful moral examples to Muslims of what it means to strive for a good end.

If we Christians knew our New Testament in an Arabic version (as Arab Christians do), we'd see that Jihad—in the sense of the Greater Jihad—plays a very similar role for us as well. In Arabic versions of the New Testament "Jihad" is used to translates a Greek word that means "struggle competitively, as in a game or in battle." It is a word especially dear to Saint Paul, whose use of it is not so different from the Qur'an's.

COMPARING THE BIBLE AND THE QUR'AN

The Texts
THE BIBLE
Luke 22:13-11
Then an angel from heaven appeared to him and gave him strength. In his anguish he prayed more earnestly, and his sweat became like great drops of blood falling down on the ground.

1 Timothy 4:7-10
Have nothing to do with profane myths and old wives' tales. Train yourself in godliness, for, while physical training is of some value, godliness is valuable in every way, holding promise for both the present life and the life to come. The saying is sure and worthy of full acceptance. For to this end we toil and struggle, because we have our hope set on the living God, who is the Savior of all people, especially of those who believe.

Philippians 1:29-30
For he has graciously granted you the privilege not only of believing in Christ, but of suffering for him as well—since you are having the same struggle that you saw I had and now hear that I still have.

THE QUR'AN
sura yusuf "Joseph" 12:1-7, 16-18
12:1These are the signs and verses of the clearest of books. 12:2We have sent it down as a Qur'an or Reciting in Arabic so that all of you may grow in wisdom and understanding. 12:3For we will tell you, Muhammad, the most beautiful of all stories in this portion of the Qur'an. Prior to this, you too were among those who are ignorant, negligent.

12:4See! Joseph said to his father Jacob, "Father, I saw eleven stars and the sun and the moon. I saw them all bow down to me!" 12:5Jacob replied, "My dear youngest son, don't tell what you saw to your brothers! If you do, they will hatch a plot against you. For Satan is a confessed enemy to humankind. ¹²⁶This is how it will happen—Your Cherisher and Sustainer will choose you, and he will teach you the interpretation of signs and stories. And he will bring his favor to perfection in you and in my descendants, just as he did in your forefathers Abraham and Isaac. For your Cherisher and Sustainer is all-knowing, wise in everything."

¹²⁷Pay attention! In the story of Joseph and his brothers there are signs for those who seek after truth....

[Jacob bends to his sons'—Joseph's brothers'—accusation that he does not trust them to take Joseph with them while they tend their sheep and reluctantly lets Joseph go. The brothers are consumed by envy. At first they want to kill Joseph, but then decide to throw him into a well.]

¹²¹⁶Then the brothers came back to their father after sundown. They were weeping. ¹²¹⁷They said, "Father, we went out of camp to run races with each other, leaving Joseph behind with our belongings. Then—a wolf ate him! But you will not believe us even though we're telling the truth!" ¹²¹⁸They had stained Joseph's shirt with false blood, the blood of a goat. Jacob said, "No, no—you have made up a story that suits yourselves. Patience—beautiful patience is my path. God alone is the best refuge against your tales."

GUIDED DISCUSSION QUESTIONS

1. *Is patience the key ingredient of the Greater Jihad?*
I once asked a young Muslim why *sura yusuf* was important to him. He immediately quoted Jacob's exclamation in verse 18: "Beautiful patience!" "I love to think about this phrase," the young man said. "Whenever I'm faced with difficulties or frustrations, that phrase and all the examples in this *sura* that illustrate it keep me strong and help me remember to trust God." The examples he was referring to are those given not only here

and elsewhere by Jacob, but also by Joseph as he patiently endures the treachery of his brothers and, later on in Egypt, the false accusation by Potiphar's wife. Joseph triumphs in the end, not through bloody revenge on his brothers, but through charity and forgiveness. (The value of patience is brought out more strongly in the Qur'an's version of Joseph's story than in the Bible's.)

Given what has already been said about the Greater Jihad, can you see why patience is a key ingredient of it?

2. What does the Greater Jihad have to do with "interpretation"?
A key statement about Joseph is made by his father Jacob in verse 6 of *sura yusuf:* "and he will teach you the interpretation of signs and stories." This happens even sooner than Jacob imagines. Right at the bottom of the well where the brothers hurl him, Joseph hears God speak the following words to his heart: "You shall one day reveal to them the meaning of this affair about which they know nothing" (12:15). So what would ordinarily look like the most hopeless of situations is transformed by Joseph's just-revealed capacity to see the event as a "sign" and to interpret it correctly. This is the beginning of Joseph's history as an interpreter of signs of all kinds, including the signs revealed in dreams.

Do you see now why the capacity for interpreting of signs would be another key ingredient of the Greater Jihad? How would patience be connected with this capacity?

3. Is Christ a Greater Jihadist?
When Arabic speakers come to the phrase translated from the original Greek of Luke 22:44 ("In his anguish…"), they see the Arabic word *jihadi.* That's because the word Jihad in its various forms translates the Greek word *agonizomai,* from *agon,* meaning "place of assembly; place of contest; stadium; the conflict itself"

(at first litigation and debate, later any conflict, including battle); also the state of mind associated with struggle, i.e., fear and "anguish." The Greek word translated "anguish" is a form of *agonizomai*.

Can you now see the sense in which Christ, in his agony in the garden, is both practicing and experiencing the Greater Jihad?

4. Is Paul a Greater Jihadist?

By far the greatest use in Arabic translations of the New Testament of the word Jihad (translating forms of *agonizomai*) occurs in Saint Paul's letters. (Other Arabic words translate the related language that Saint Paul uses for athletic striving of all kinds, especially boxing, racing and even gladiatorial combat.)

Take a look at the examples from 1 Timothy and Philippians. Can you find the English words that are translated in Arabic by forms of the word Jihad? (Second Timothy 4:7 and Colossians 2:1 give other examples you can check out.) What meaning or meanings of Jihad are expressed in these examples?

Why is it that Jihad (and related words for striving) is used so frequently by Saint Paul (as well as by the writer of Hebrews) while it is used only once in the Arabic gospels, and then only, as we've seen, of Jesus himself? Why is it never used in Gospel accounts of the disciples' behavior?

5. How does reflecting on the Greater Jihad help us see how "grace" means different things to Muslims and Christians?

In the introduction to this chapter I stated that "according to the Qur'an we come into the world fully equipped with God's favor or grace." The Greater Jihad is the proper human response to this gift. There is no excuse for not "striving for a good end."

We Christians would not see grace—or the Christian Jihad that responds to it—in quite the same light. Why not? How and why is grace given to us as opposed to how and why it is given to Muslims? Recall what we discovered in chapter six of this book: that the Qur'an's Adam and Eve, once having been caused to "slip" from the Garden, afterward repent and are forgiven by God. There is no "Fall" as we Christians understand it. How does this fact affect the Muslim conception of grace, giving it a different dimension from its Christian counterpart?

CHAPTER FIFTEEN

WHAT DO WE EACH BELIEVE ABOUT THE LESSER JIHAD?

Introduction

The word *Jihad*, as our Western media tends to use it, occupies about the same place in our American imagination as the word "Communism" did back during the Cold War. Both words are scare words: words that provoke fear, panic and a determination to divide the world into "us" and "them" with "good" on our side and "evil" on theirs.

This is not to say that yesterday's Soviets and today's Muslim terrorists were not and are not cause for great concern and measures of self-defense. It is to say that acts of hostility among nations (or between a nation and a terrorist group) always have long and complicated histories. Without knowing that history, we can't rightly judge the present. And without judging the present rightly, we can't rightly deal with it. We become prisoners of our frightened reaction.

Jihad is a case in point. Our fear prevents us from seeing that it is not a simple concept in Islam. As the Greater Jihad—the striving to master the self—very closely resembles key ideas in the Gospels and in the letters of Saint Paul, the Lesser Jihad—a striving to defend the community—very closely resembles ideas of the Just War elaborated in the fifth century by Saint Augustine and by other Christian thinkers since. The Lesser Jihad, according to the Qur'an and the *hadith*—the prime sources of Muslim self-understanding—has nothing to do with terrorism, with the assault on innocent lives as a means to call attention to grievances. The Qur'an and *hadith* explicitly condemn such behavior, and Muslim tradition has upheld the condemnation.

Readers can judge for themselves whether the Qur'an endorses Jihad as terrorism by reflecting on the following passage from *sura at-tauba*. The word Jihad itself does not appear until verse 16. In the lines before that, the Qur'an describes conflicts the young Muslim community was having both with pagan Bedouin tribes in Medina (where Muhammad had taken his followers during the *hijrah* or emigration) and with pagan Meccans back in Mecca itself. It is to certain of these lines that people today often refer when they want to show that Islam is a violent religion. This context, they say, supports the interpretation of Jihad in verse 16 (and elsewhere) as justifying violence, so that Jihad, for them, becomes synonymous with Holy War.

Even if readers decide that Jihad, as used in *sura at-tauba*, does not equal terrorism or "Holy War," they may still compare Islam unfavorably with Christianity by pointing out that the New Testament does not endorse warfare, not even the so-called Just War (although in certain places it advocates praying for and obeying the emperor). It is true that Christianity did not develop a concept of the Lesser Jihad during its first two centuries. But when Constantine, before the Battle of the Milvian Bridge in AD 315, saw in a dream a cross in the sky bearing the motto "By this sign you conquer," our faith began to take what had previously been symbols of spiritual battle and put them on hard shields and helmets, thereby declaring that its armies were doing God's will.

And so began Christianity's Lesser Jihad.

The Texts
THE BIBLE
Ephesians 6:10–17

Finally, be strong in the Lord and in the strength of his power. Put on the whole armor of God, so that you may be able to stand against the wiles of the devil. For our struggle is not against enemies of blood and flesh, but against the rulers, against the authorities, against the cosmic powers of this present darkness, against the spiritual forces of evil in the heavenly places. Therefore take up the whole armor of God, so that you may be able to withstand on that evil day, and having done everything, to stand firm. Stand therefore, and fasten the belt of truth around your waist, and put on the breastplate of righteousness. As shoes for your feet put on whatever will make you ready to proclaim the gospel of peace. With all of these, take the shield of faith, with which you will be able to quench all the flaming arrows of the evil one. Take the helmet of salvation, and the sword of the Spirit, which is the word of God.

THE QUR'AN
sura at-tauba "Repentance" 9:1–16

9:1A treaty of immunity from God and his messenger Muhammad to those among the pagan Bedouin tribes with whom you have made alliances: 9:2Go anywhere you want throughout the earth, you idolaters [i.e., pagan Bedouin tribes], for four months, but be aware that God will not be fooled by your treachery. Rather, God will bring shame on those who deny him.

9:3And an announcement from God and his messenger to the people gathered on the day of the Great Hajj to Mecca: that

God is freed of all connection with idolaters at Mecca itself—and his messenger is freed as well. Even then, you idolaters, if you turn in repentance to God, it will be best for you. But if you turn away, be aware that you cannot fool God. So announce to those who deny God a terrible consequence.

9:4All this shall happen except to those idolaters with whom you have made alliances and who since then have never betrayed you in any way, nor given aid behind your back to enemies. 9:5But when the four months are over and the other party has persisted in its treachery, then fight the idolaters wherever you find them. Seize them, beset them, besiege them, wait for them in ambush. Yet still—if they repent, if they observe daily prayer, if they give to the poor, then clear the way for them. Remember that God is all-forgiving, most merciful.

9:6And if one of the idolaters seeks you out for protection, then grant it to him, so that he may hear the word of God. Afterward, escort him to a safe place. Such things happen because they are a people without knowledge of God.

9:7How can there be an alliance with idolaters in God's sight and in the sight of the messenger, except for those with whom you made alliances near the Sacred Mosque in Mecca? As long as they stand firm in their commitment to you, do the same with them. Remember that God loves those who are attentive to him and him alone.

9:8But again, how can there be an alliance with idolaters since, if they get the better of you in some way, they respect neither kinship ties nor treaties? They please you with their mouths, uttering friendly phrases, but in their hearts they scorn you. The greater part of them are transgressors, they know no bounds. 9:9They have sold God's words for a trifle and have hindered others from God's way. Their deeds are in every way evil. 9:10They do not respect kinship ties with a believer—nor treaties either. Clearly it is they who have transgressed all bounds.

9:11Yet–if they repent, if they keep regular prayers, if they give alms, then they shall become your brothers in worship. This is how we explain our signs to a people who understand.

9:12But if they violate their trust after they make their treaties with you, if they mock you for your faithfulness, then fight those great exemplars of faithlessness! Their word means nothing to them. So fight them–perhaps they will learn to restrain themselves.

9:13Will you not fight a people who has violated its trust? Who are plotting even now to expel the messenger from Medina? Didn't they attack you first? What? Are you afraid of them? Yet it is more reasonable to fear God if you are true believers.

9:14So, fight them! Using your hands, God will punish them, he will cover them with shame, he will help you overcome them. And God will heal believers' hearts of all injury caused by violence. 9:15For he will remove their fury and give them peace. God turns in mercy to whomever he pleases. Remember that God is all-knowing, all-wise.

9:16Or did you hope that you would be let alone? That God would not test you to learn who among you practices Jihad? To learn who among you counts no one his intimate friend but God and his messenger and the other believers? Remember that God is very much aware of everything you do.

GUIDED DISCUSSION QUESTIONS

1. *What explanation can be given about the tone of* sura at-tauba? We have no "objective" way of judging the disputes referred to in this excerpt from *sura at-tauba*. We lack, that is, any direct evidence about what the Bedouin tribes at Medina or what the pagan Meccans thought about the Qur'an's accusation that the majority of them were incapable or unwilling to abide by their

word in treaties with Muhammad's new community of Muslims. All our information about the disputes comes from the Qur'an itself.

Leaving that issue aside, however, what do you think about the tone of this excerpt? Remember that it is to certain lines of this passage that people refer when they want to show that Islam is a violent religion. Would you describe the overall tone as inciting to violence?

2. *Where is the "Sword" in the "Sword Verse"?*
You can focus this question by examining verse 5 of the *sura at-tauba*. Traditionally called the "Sword Verse" (although the word "sword" does not appear in it), this verse is one of those most frequently cited in proof of Islam's inherent violence. Does that name seem appropriate?

Usually when this line is cited, it is cited by opponents of Islam only in part—only up to "Yet still—...." What explanation might you give as to why it tends to be abbreviated in this way?

3. *Is this an odd way of securing a treaty?*
Among Bedouin tribes of Muhammad's day, the way to secure a treaty was to exchange hostages: valuable objects, valuable people, even one's own person. But that is not what the Qur'an seems to be requiring. Take the "Sword Verse" itself. What it requires of the idolaters to secure their word is that they observe daily prayer and give to the poor. (Verse 11 says the same thing.)

Why do you suppose the Qur'an judges such behavior to be enough? Go back to the discussion of the word "Islam" in chapter one, particularly to the word's original meaning among the Bedouins and then to the Qur'an's transformation of the word.

4. *Is Jihad a command to kill?*
Note that we finally arrive at the word *Jihad* in verse 16, at the

COMPARING THE BIBLE AND THE QUR'AN

climax of what the previous lines say about how to deal with treacherous idolaters.

What meaning should we give to Jihad within its context? Should we restrict its meaning in verse 16 to killing? Is the Qur'an saying that simply by killing idolaters we are showing that we are God's "intimate friend"?

5. Is Saint Paul advocating Holy War?

A citizen of the Roman Empire and a fluent writer of Greek, Saint Paul readily employed every persuasive tactic he could to encourage the young Gentile communities to follow Christ alone and Christ crucified. War-making language made up a key part of the Gentile vocabulary, and Saint Paul readily and comfortably employed it, as the quotation from Ephesians demonstrates. Examples abound in Saint Paul's letter to the Philippians as well (see Philippians 1:27–2:18, for instance). Of course Saint Paul makes clear that he envisions warfare in a spiritual rather than a physical sense. Nevertheless, the military language he uses in Ephesians, Philippians and elsewhere resembles very closely the speeches we possess from that era of generals haranguing their troops before battle.

Think about the language of battle used in Ephesians, in Philippians and in Revelation (a New Testament book not by Paul). Then, if you have time, refer to a good contemporary history of the Crusades. (Thomas Asbridge's *The First Crusade: A New History* is a reliable and accessible resource.) See if you can find examples of the language used by Pope Urban II to justify sending Christian knights to the Holy Land beginning in AD 1095. What has happened in Urban's speeches to the concept of a purely spiritual battle described by Paul in Ephesians?

Your discussions might probe more recent uses of God's name in support of "Christian knights" against "godless" enemies.

CHAPTER SIXTEEN

WHAT DO WE EACH BELIEVE ABOUT THE JUDGMENT?

Introduction

Judgment as presented in the Qur'an and in the New Testament looks pretty much the same. A trumpet will blow, the old earth will be destroyed, and the new one will be inaugurated by the accounting each of us, Muslims and Christians alike, will have to give before an all-knowing Judge.

A deeper investigation reveals the differences. One difference is that the Qur'an talks about Judgment more often than the New Testament does. Judgment is a subject in almost every one of the Qur'an's *suras*, and it is usually painted in dramatic detail. In the following excerpt, we learn only that a Book of Deeds is presented to God and that the prophets and angelic witnesses are called in to testify. Other *suras* tell more about the roles the angelic witnesses play. Two angels follow us throughout our adult lives, one of them noting with unfailing accuracy our good deeds, the other with the same precision our failings and transgressions. These angels will lay open their accounts at Judgment for minute inspection. But that is not all. We ourselves will be called to testify, though not in speech. Our mouths will be sealed in order to muzzle our excuses and self-justifications. In their place, our hands and our feet—and in one *sura* even our very skins—will "speak" for or against us, reenacting all that we did in life down to the last and most shameful—or honorable—detail. As the Qur'an puts it:

> Whoever has done the tiniest bit of good will see it.
> Whoever has done the tiniest bit of evil will see it.
> (*sura al-zilzal* "The Quaking")

But perhaps the most significant difference is in the role played by Jesus. In one place the Qur'an indicates that the prophet Jesus will return just before the Last Judgment to usher it in. But he will be judged at that time just like everyone else. For us Christians, however, Jesus in his role as Son of Man is the Judge. Even more, Jesus is also the Judgment, in so far as our deeds done or not done to the "least of these" in the Gospel of Matthew are done or not done to him. Exploring this difference in Jesus' role at Judgment is a key challenge for interfaith understanding.

The Texts
THE BIBLE
Matthew 25:31–46

When the Son of Man comes in his glory, and all the angels with him, then he will sit on the throne of his glory. All the nations will be gathered before him, and he will separate people one from another as a shepherd separates the sheep from the goats, and he will put the sheep at his right hand and the goats at the left. Then the king will say to those at his right hand, "Come, you that are blessed by my Father, inherit the kingdom prepared for you from the foundation of the world; for I was hungry and you gave me food, I was thirsty and you gave me something to drink, I was a stranger and you welcomed me, I was naked and you gave me clothing, I was sick and you took care of me, I was in prison and you visited me." Then the righteous will answer him, "Lord, when was it that we saw you hungry and gave you food, or thirsty and gave you something to drink? And when was it that we saw you a stranger and welcomed you, or naked and gave you clothing? And when was it that we saw you sick or in prison and visited you?" And the king will answer them, "Truly I tell you, just as you did it to one of the least of these who are members of my family, you did it to me." Then he will say to those at his left hand, "You that are accursed, depart from me into the eternal fire prepared for the devil and his angels; for I was hungry and you gave me no food, I was thirsty and you gave me nothing to drink, I was a stranger and you did not welcome me, naked and you did not give me clothing, sick and in prison you did not visit me." Then they also will answer, "Lord, when was it that we saw you hungry or thirsty or a stranger or naked or sick or in prison, and did not take care of you?" Then he will answer them, "Truly I tell you, just as you did not do it to one of the least of these, you did not do it to me." And these will go away into eternal punishment, but the righteous into eternal life.

THE QUR'AN

sura al-zumar "The Crowds" 39:67–75

[39:67]The transgressors have not taken God's measure wisely, for on the Day of Judgment the earth and all that is in it will be squeezed in God's palm and the heavens rolled up in his right hand. Glory to him! He is high, far above the partners they associate to him. [39:68]Then the trumpet shall sound, and all that are in heaven and all that are on the earth will faint away except those whom God exempts. Then the trumpet will sound a second time and—behold!—they will all now be standing, watching expectantly. [39:69]And the earth will shine in the light of her Cherisher and Sustainer, and the Book of each person's deeds will be placed in God's hands, and the prophets will approach along with unimpeachable angelic witnesses, and among them the Judgment will be just and fair, nor will anyone be wronged. 39:70For each person will be judged according to his or her deeds. God knows unerringly what they have done.

39:71And those who refused to believe will be driven to Hell in crowds until, when they arrive, Hell's gates will be opened and Hell's angelic keepers will say to them, "Didn't messengers arise from among you to point out to you the signs of your Cherisher and Sustainer and to warn you of the Meeting on this, your own day?" Other angels will say in reply, "Yes, the messengers arose and spoke, but now has come the Word of punishment upon those who disbelieved." 39:72Then it will be said to the Hell-bound, "Pass through Hell's gates and dwell inside. Evil is this place for those who were arrogant and made idols of themselves."

39:73But those who feared their Cherisher and Sustainer will be led to the Garden in crowds until, when they arrive there, the gates to the Garden will be opened and the Garden's angelic keepers will say, "*Salaamun aleikum!* Peace and fullness be upon you! You have pleased God. Enter the Garden and dwell inside."

39:74The Garden-bound will say, "All praise to God who has fulfilled his covenant with us. He has given us this land as an inheritance, and we may dwell in the Garden wherever we wish." Surely this is the best of all possible rewards for those who do good deeds.

39:75And you will see the angels going round about God's throne, giving glory and praise to their Cherisher and Sustainer. And the Judgment will be just and fair, and all will cry out, "All praise to God, Cherisher and Sustainer of the worlds!"

GUIDED DISCUSSION QUESTIONS

1. *Do Muslims believe in the resurrection of the body?*
Let's take a second look at verse 68 from the excerpt of the Qur'an:

> Then the trumpet shall sound, and all that are in heaven and all
> that are on the earth will faint and fall away except those whom
> God exempts. Then the trumpet will sound a second time and–
> behold!–they will all now be standing, watching expectantly.

We might be tempted to say that resurrection is being described here. There is the sudden end of all physical life and of our physical bodies. An interval of annihilation follows (the "fainting and falling away"). Then comes a re-creation of ourselves in imperishable physical form, awaiting Judgment. As for Jesus– known as 'Isa in the Qur'an–he will be recreated in this way along with the rest of us. Yet the Christian Jesus' own resurrection after his death on the cross plays absolutely no role in the transformation described by the Qur'an. (As we saw in chapter nine, the Qur'an denies that Jesus died on the cross in the first place.)

Is "resurrection" a word you're comfortable using of the transformation described in verse 68?

2. *What do the criteria of Muslim and Christian Judgment have in common?*
Consider the warning Jesus makes earlier in Matthew 12:36–37: "I tell you, on the day of judgment you will have to give an account for every careless word you utter; for by your words you will be justified and by your words you will be condemned." Take a look at the context in which Jesus says this (especially Matthew 12:34–35) to get a feeling for the behavior Jesus is warning against.

How might Jesus' warning in Matthew 12:36–37 relate to the kind of Judgment given by the prophets and angelic witnesses in the excerpt given from the Qur'an?

3. What is the Muslim objection to Jesus as Judge and Judgment?
When Jesus says in Matthew 25:31–46 that the criterion for salvation is whether we have fed the hungry, he is saying what the Qur'an says as well when it talks (as it does repeatedly) about the obligation of taking care of widows, orphans and the poor. The difference, as we said in the introduction to this chapter, has to do with Jesus' role in establishing and upholding the criterion. The Qur'an would never say that Jesus ever played or still could play such extremely diverse roles: the role of Judge and that of the very body of suffering humanity.

Why would the Qur'an never claim such things about Jesus? (To help answer this question, you may want to reread chapters nine and ten for the Qur'an's distinction between Jesus and 'Isa.)

4. According to Matthew 25:31–46, would Muslims be as likely as Christians to be found among the sheep at Jesus' right hand?
Matthew 25:40 makes clear that at Judgment deeds will speak louder than words: "Truly I tell you, just as you did it to one of the least of these who are members of my family, you did it to me."

The criterion for determining whether a person will be among the sheep at Jesus' right hand or among the goats at his left is whether his or her concern for the poor and marginalized (the "least" of the members of Jesus' "family") has been active. And also whether the person's concern has been sincere— whether it has been motivated by mercy like Jesus' own rather than by expectation of reward. Or even by an awareness that it was Jesus whom he or she was serving. By contrast, those on

Jesus' left hand are "accursed" because their charity, while loudly proclaimed in Jesus' name, was performed only to receive credit from other human beings.

Given such a criterion, would you expect to see as many Muslims as Christians among the sheep at Jesus' right hand?

CHAPTER SEVENTEEN

WHAT DO WE EACH BELIEVE ABOUT
HEAVEN AND HELL?

Introduction

Muslim and Christian images of heaven and hell, like their
respective images of Judgment, look very similar on first glance.
Heaven for both religions is a place of perpetual pleasure and
rejoicing, while hell is just the opposite—a place of perpetual torment and frustration, of "weeping and gnashing of teeth," as the
Gospel of Matthew puts it in several places.

Yet a closer look reveals that the images are different. For
one thing, they are different in number and intensity. There are
many more images of heaven and hell in the Qur'an than in the
New Testament, and they are elaborated in much greater detail.
The Qur'an paints a graphic picture of what awaits us after
Judgment, while the New Testament, by comparison, seems sat-
isfied just to give hints of what is to come.

This difference doesn't mean that we Christians lack imagination or that our belief in the afterlife is less developed than
the Muslim belief. Neither, alternatively, does it mean that
Muslims have too much imagination or that they have confused
the pleasures and pains of earthly life with those of the life to

come. The difference in these images reflects a more significant difference in our understanding of our relation to God. The Qur'an's invitation is far more modest, far more restricted. It is an invitation to know and praise God and by doing so to fulfill our creaturely natures as human beings. But never, not even in heaven, do we cross the barrier that separates us from God. Christians' and Muslims' respective images of heaven and hell reflect what each religion believes to be humankind's future possibilities. That is why the Qur'an, as in passages like the one that follows, emphasizes the sensed details of reward and punishment. Heaven and hell are close approximations to the best and worst that human life here and now can offer. The New Testament, by contrast, speaks of a future unity with God utterly unimaginable to us, even though we have been given a foretaste of it even in this life. "Beloved, we are God's children now," as the writer of the first letter of John puts it. "[W]hat we will be has not yet been revealed. What we do know is this: when he is revealed, we will be like him, for we will see him as he is" (1 John 3:2).

As sensuous as the details of the Qur'anic heaven and hell are, however, they still function morally. The physical delights and torments awaiting us in the Qur'anic heaven or in the Qur'anic hell are expressions of a fulfilled relationship between ourselves and God and between ourselves and other people. Muslims and Christians do not differ over the desirability of the fulfillment (or over the horror of the fulfillment's opposite). Where we differ is in the fulfillment's extent and depth.

The Texts
THE BIBLE
Matthew 25:30

As for this worthless slave, throw him into the outer darkness, where there will be weeping and gnashing of teeth.

Revelation 19:20; 21:2; 22:1–5

And the beast was captured, and with it the false prophet who had performed in its presence the signs by which he deceived those who had received the mark of the beast and those who worshipped its image. These two were thrown alive into the lake of fire that burns with sulphur....

And I saw the holy city, the new Jerusalem, coming down out of heaven from God, prepared as a bride adorned for her husband....

Then the angel showed me the river of the water of life, bright as crystal, flowing from the throne of God and of the Lamb through the middle of the street of the city. On either side of the river is the tree of life with its twelve kinds of fruit, producing its fruit each month; and the leaves of the tree are for the healing of the nations. Nothing accursed will be found there any more. But the throne of God and of the Lamb will be in it, and his servants will worship him; they will see his face, and his name will be on their foreheads. And there will be no more night; they need no light of lamp or sun, for the Lord God will be their light, and they will reign forever and ever.

THE QUR'AN
sura waqi'ah "What Is Coming" 56:7–56

56:7When the old creation crumbles away and the new one comes into being, you will be separated into three groups.

56:8First will come the Companions of the Right Hand. Who are the Companions of the Right Hand? 56:9Next will come the Companions of the Left Hand. Who are the Companions of the Left hand? 56:10And finally will come the Foremost in faith, who will be Foremost in Heaven.

56:11For these Foremost ones will take places nearest to God 56:12in Gardens of joy, 56:13many of them from the people of olden times, 56:14and a few from more recent ones. 56:15They will sit on chairs inlaid with precious stones, [56:16]resting on them and facing each other conversationally. [56:17]And moving around them, serving them, will be young men, perpetually attentive, [56:18]bearing bowls, shining pitchers, and cups brimming with spring water. [56:19]There will be no hangovers from their feast, no drunkenness. [56:20]They shall taste fruits, any that they choose, [56:21]and the flesh of fowl, whatever they desire. [56:22]They shall have female companions with black eyes, [56:23]companions like well-guarded pearls, [56:24]their reward for their deeds in their past life. [56:25]In that Garden there will be no foolish talk, no malicious gossip, [56:26]but only the words "Peace! Peace!"

[56:27]Now for the Companions of the Right Hand. Who are the Companions of the Right Hand? [56:28]They will rest among lote-trees shorn of their thorns [56:29]and shrubs bearing tiers of flowers [56:30]under spreading shade [56:31]near fresh, flowing water [56:32]with fruit in abundance, [56:33]always in season, never denied.

[56:34]And on seats raised high [56:35]we have brought into being their female companions, [56:36]making them fresh as the morning, [56:37]beloved wives of the Companions' same age, [56:38]all these for the Companions of the Right Hand, [56:39]a large number from the people of olden times, [56:40]but a large number too from people of more recent ones.

[56:41]Then, finally, come the Companions of the Left Hand. Who are the Companions of the Left Hand? [56:42]You will find them in the hot blast, in the boiling water, [56:43]and in the shade of black smoke—[56:44]not at all cooling or refreshing! [56:45]For in former times they lived the good life to the hilt, [56:46]stubbornly persisting in the greediest self-sufficiency. [56:47]They used to say with a sneer, "Ahah! So when we die and turn to dust and bones, you claim we will be raised up again? [56:48]What? Our fathers and our ancestors too?" [56:49]Say this in reply to them: "Yes, and not only your ancestors, but all those before them as well. [56:50]Every single one of them will be gathered for the Meeting on the appointed Day. ⁵⁶:⁵¹Then for sure, O you who willfully go astray and deny the truth, ⁵⁶:⁵²then you will eat of the Poison Tree at the bottom of Hell, ⁵⁶:⁵³you will fill your bellies with it, ⁵⁶:⁵⁴and afterward you will drink boiling water to wash it down ⁵⁶:⁵⁵like diseased she-camels raging with thirst!"

⁵⁶:⁵⁶That will be their "entertainment" on the Day!

GUIDED DISCUSSION QUESTIONS

1. *In what way have Christian and Muslim images of hell and heaven been influenced by culture and geography?*
We shouldn't be surprised that the images of heaven found in Revelation are urban. The writer of Revelation was a city-dweller speaking to other city-dwellers. That is why, at the end of things, we enter a "holy city, a new Jerusalem." The images of hell derive from the Valley of Gehenna near Jerusalem where children used to be burned alive to Moloch.

Compare these images with the Qur'an's. What do you know about Mecca and environs during prophet Muhammad's time that might help you understand why the Qur'an makes such frequent mention of water and gardens in referring to heaven and of smoke and fire in referring to hell?

2. *For what are the Companions of the Left Hand being punished?*
The Companions of the Left Hand were the clan leaders of the Quraysh tribe, who ruled Mecca and derived profit from the *hajj* traffic. (See chapter one.) They pretended to cling to the Bedouin belief in a tribal god. According to this belief, the god watches over the well-being of the tribe but offers no life after death. After one's death, life continues in the tribe itself. And given the harsh circumstances of desert existence, the tribes gave great value to every member, especially the male ones. But when the Quraysh started to become a settled community in

Mecca, certain individuals among them began to get rich thanks to the increasing caravan trade. Mores and morals began changing, and for the worse. You can see the nasty direction things were taking from the accusation that the Companions were "stubbornly persisting in the greediest self-sufficiency."

Put in your own words what crime or crimes are being hinted at here. How would you name the positive virtues to which the Qur'an is opposing these crimes?

3. Is there an orgy in heaven awaiting for pious Muslim men?
The references in the Qur'anic passage and in others like them to "female companions" (the "rewards" of the just) seem to support the view that Islam is a religion just for men and especially for the sensualists among them. Muslims take great offense at this characterization, regarding it as prejudiced in the extreme. They regard the inclusion of the female companions as a sign of the fulfillment awaiting all human relationships in heaven, men's and women's both.

What details in the description of the Qur'anic heaven can you find that would support the Muslim view?

Chapter Eighteen

What Do We Each Believe About God?

Introduction

Do we worship the same God? We have skirted this book's central question in the previous chapters. Now it is time to confront it directly.

The passages chosen to focus our question are the ones that most believers of either religion would probably cite as the central scriptural formulations of what their respective faiths tell them about God. For Christians, that passage would be John 3:16. For Muslims, it would be *sura al-ikhlas* "Purity."

Both passages have the advantage of brevity.

Both are easily memorized.

Both are often singled out for special display within worship spaces. Sometimes, as in the case of John 3:16, they are boldly broadcast to the world—recall the John 3:16 signs held up by pious fans at sports events for the benefit of the TV cameras.

Both also take an uncompromising stand on exactly who God is and what God does—or does not do.

Both challenge a previous stand on those same points. The passage from John is the one in which Jesus directly challenges the orthodox monotheistic belief of Nicodemus, a Pharisee and the member of the Jewish Sanhedrin who "came to Jesus by night" (John 3:2). John 3:16 asserts that God actually begot and sent a Son to save us. Similarly, *sura al-ikhlas* directly challenges the very language of John 3:16!

Here is where, as they say, "the rubber hits the road." If throughout his nocturnal conversation with Nicodemus Jesus begins to sway the fearful Nicodemus from the rigid belief that attributing a Son to God is blasphemy, *al-ikhlas* attempts to bring belief in one God back to its strict monotheistic starting point. Not to its starting point among the Jews, however, who in the Qur'an's eyes have betrayed their trust in God as One by their divisive behavior. And most emphatically not to the Christian redefinition of belief in God as belief in the Son whom he sent. *Al-ikhlas* attempts to bring belief in God back to the original divine revelation itself, now restored in its purity through the Qur'an, or Reciting, handed down through the prophet Muhammad.

But if John 3:16 and *al-ikhlas* compete as accounts of who God is, what can it mean to say, as the popes and bishops of Vatican II did, that we worship the same God? Aren't Christianity and Islam on opposite sides of this question? How can we say we worship the same God as Muslims do when the Qur'an explicitly denies Jesus as Son? How could the popes and bishops have been mistaken on such a vital point?

Yet, on further thought, to call those popes and bishops "mistaken" goes too far. Those who have had the time to work through the previous chapters of this book will, I hope, acknowledge that up to this point our central question about God hasn't allowed an easy answer, either in favor of the popes' and bishops' assessment at Vatican II or against it. It doesn't allow one here, either, not even when comparing passages from

John and *al-ikhlas* that seem to say opposite things about God. Just when we think that "no!" is the only answer to "Do we worship the same God?" grounds for thinking otherwise begin to emerge, and a "yes!" becomes more and more possible.

Alas for us if we thought that the question, "Do we worship the same God?" could be wrapped up with a neat answer and put away safely on a high shelf! The question continues to challenge us. May we have the patience to let the challenge work within us, a spur to greater understanding and a motive for deeper faith.

The Texts:
THE BIBLE
John 3:16

For God so loved the world that he gave his only Son, so that everyone who believes in him may not perish but may have eternal life.

THE QUR'AN
sura al-ikhlas "Purity" 112:1–4

112:1Say, O Muhammad: "He, God, is One. 112:2God is eternal, self-sufficient. 112:3He does not beget offspring, nor was he begotten. 112:4To him there is absolutely nothing comparable."

GUIDED DISCUSSION QUESTIONS
1. *Do these passages have something in common?*
John 3:16 and *al-ikhlas* actually have a lot in common, at least implicitly.

Look at what is said about God in suras 1, 2 and 4. Do you see God described in those verses in ways that you would say are incompatible with Christian belief? What are your reasons for thinking so—or for coming to the opposite conclusion (that those ways are not incompatible with Christian belief)?

2. Is God in al-ikhlas *not as remote as he might seem?*
Even if we agree that the attributes given to God in verses 1, 2 and 4 of *al-ikhlas*—his oneness, his eternalness, his self-sufficiency, his incomparableness—are not incompatible with Christian belief, we might still say that to emphasize those attributes is to project a God who is cold and remote, not the loving God we know in Jesus Christ.

Yet what happens to this impression when we take into account the fact that *sura al-ikhlas*, like every other *sura* in the Qur'an except for one, is preceded by the *bismillah,* or the formula, "In the name of God, the most beneficent, the most merciful"? As when we cross ourselves, the *bismillah* identifies a person as a worshiper of the God of Abraham—Christians under the sign of the cross, Muslims under the sign of God's chief attributes, benevolence and mercy. ("Benevolence" refers to God's generosity in creating the world in the first place. "Mercy" refers to his infinitely tender care of that Creation once made.) What the *bismillah* says is that while God is supremely transcendent in the ways *al-ikhlas* specifies, he is also, in the famous phrase from *sura qaf* 50:16, closer to us "than our jugular vein."

Keeping in mind Islam's strong emphasis on God's care and concern in the *bismillah* and other Qur'anic passages (many of them already discussed in this book), how willing would you be to back someone up who insisted that the "Muslim God" is a cold-hearted tyrant, the very reverse of a God of love?

3. Is verse 3 of al-ikhlas *as decisively anti-Christian as it seems to be?*
The collision point in *al-ikhlas* for Christians and Muslims is verse 3, because it's there that belief in a Son of God is emphatically denied. And in fact the claim in verse 3 that God "does not beget offspring, nor was he begotten" is usually understood by Muslim scholars and clerics to refute Christian creedal language about God's "begotten" Son. The scholars and clerics support

their refutation by pointing out that since God is not a physical being like ourselves, he would never have fathered a son as human beings do. The scholars and clerics insist that to assert otherwise is to commit the blasphemy of confusing the creator with his creation. In a word, idolatry.

Let us take a deep breath and think carefully about what this supposedly anti-Christian verse is actually saying. Isn't there something odd about this verse? Would we Christians not actually agree with the Muslim scholars and clerics? Would we not actually join them in refuting the notion that God "fathered" a son in the physical sense intended? When Gabriel announces to Mary in Luke 1:35 that the Holy Spirit "will come upon you, and the power of the Most High will overshadow you," no Christian—and no Muslim—believes that Gabriel is talking about sexual congress, as in Greek legends where Zeus took the form of a bull to impregnate Europa or the form of a swan to impregnate Leda. And as for the language about "begetting," the Councils of Nicaea in AD 325 and Constantinople in AD 381 were dedicated in great part to stripping from the word "beget" when used of God every imputation of creatureliness.

Based on what you now know about what verse 3 of *al-ikhlas* is saying, how anti-Christian is it?

4. Do we worship the same God?

It begins to look as if verse 3 of *al-ikhlas* is actually refuting a belief about God—the belief that God impregnated Mary sexually—that we find just as heretical as Muslims do. But if that is so, aren't we entitled to draw the conclusion that Christian and Muslim differences about God are based more on misunderstandings than on realities? This does seem to be a tempting possibility. Tempting because once we've drawn that conclusion, our job would seem pretty much over. All we have to do is sit down with our Muslim brothers and sisters to clear up the misunderstanding about God's relations with Mary and, as if by magic, all is well. We *do* worship the same God. Case closed.

But no, it just is not that easy. Our agreeing what God did *not* do (i.e., impregnate Mary) does not mean we agree on what God *did* do (i.e., beget a Son). But beyond even that: Having worked through the various scriptural comparisons presented in this book, we are aware that Christian and Muslim differences are real. Just as real as our similarities. It is not a question either for us or for Muslims of swinging from one extreme to another (from saying our religions are incompatible to saying that they are simply two versions of the same thing). The differences and similarities must be honored. Whether we worship the same God or not cannot be resolved hastily or prematurely— yet neither must an answer be despaired of. The question is too important for that.

So, what do you think: Do we worship the same God?

CONCLUSION

Do Christians and Muslims worship the same God?

It is likely that different answers to our key question have been reached by each of the different groups or individuals who have faithfully worked through most or all of this book's eighteen chapters. None of the answers reached is the "right" one—or the only right one. The magnitude of the question—it is God we are talking about, after all!—doesn't allow us the satisfaction of simple certainty. Of course, the answer has already been given in the resounding "yes!" from the popes and bishops of Vatican II. Church teaching since then has not wavered. We are not rejecting the "yes!" given by our bishops and popes. It is rather that we have conscientiously attempted, by comparing biblical and Qur'anic texts, to live out the question more deeply.

But we have also acknowledged that by doing so we have been taking but a first step. The second step will be our inviting the Muslims in our area to live out the question along with us. Our dialogue with Islam will truly come alive and bear fruit when we engage the question with those who have even more at stake in its fullest answer than we do.

Muslims have more at stake because of the suspicion and hostility that the disaster of September 11 has brought upon them. Muslims make convenient scapegoats. Some of the ways Muslims are scapegoated are crudely obvious and, although painful, can be directly addressed—hate speech, for example, or vicious behavior. Other ways are subtler and therefore more difficult to deal with. I'm thinking about job discrimination, for example, or discrimination when seeking housing, education, social services, permanent residency status or citizenship. And then there are forms of scapegoating condoned or even perpetrated by our government under the umbrella of the so-called "war on terror." The provisions of the Patriot Act, for example, have made life difficult not only for Muslim immigrants but for Muslim Americans as well.

It is imperative that we Catholic Christians do the hard work of overcoming the poisonous effects of scapegoating. Good citizenship would require as much, to say nothing of the commandment given us to "Love your neighbor as yourself." This book has offered a starting point that provides a means for Catholic Christians to enter concretely and specifically into some of their Muslim sisters' and brothers' most cherished Qur'anic texts. By no means has this book covered everything in those texts. But it has covered enough to allow real conversation with Muslims to begin. Scapegoating finds it tough to put down roots where the social soil has been prepared and watered by genuine human exchange.

You might say in objection that you don't know any Muslims in your area. Or that while you're acquainted with a few Muslims, you don't know how to invite them into the kind of dialogue envisioned here.

As to the first objection: Although it's true that Muslims form a relatively small part of our population—probably no more than several million—their numbers are growing, and they are beginning to locate throughout the United States. Some people may not even realize that there are Muslims living in their area.

As to the second objection: What our communities lack is a church structure dedicated to bringing people of various faiths together. But there are exceptions. In Rochester, for example, Bishop Matthew Clark signed in May 2003 an agreement with Rochester's mosques pledging that both communities, Catholic and Muslim, will work together to educate each other, to combat bigotry and to promote common works of social justice. Under the aegis of such an agreement, it has been relatively easy for Catholics and Muslims to meet, befriend each other, and to talk over the kinds of questions presented in this book. In fact, the book grows directly out of dialogues I've been able to take part in with Muslim and Christian groups who have been encouraged to come together thanks to initiatives like Bishop Clark's.

What is required for such initiatives is strong, inspired leadership. Where can that leadership be found in your town or city? If no one comes to mind, then maybe the person being called forward is you!

Finally, on top of the more serious motivations to promote honest dialogue with Muslims, I have to add one more: the fun of it. My Muslim friends and I—and other Christians—have a great time together. We plan programs for the Rochester public dealing with weighty topics like "Extremism and Fundamentalism in Islam and Christianity," "Christian and Muslim Jihad," "The Seven Sacraments and the Five Pillars." But we laugh a lot as we do so, bearing down on the task at hand for a while, then interrupting things to complain about our aches and pains, then dragging ourselves back on topic, then going off on tangents about our children and grandchildren, and on and on. At other times we have meals together.

We pray together. We comfort each other when we're struggling with disease or death. In short, we behave like human beings when we're at our best—enjoying each other, seeking the best for each other and our world. This would be a joyful picture no matter what the group involved, but seasoning our fun is the knowledge that we are also enjoying our great differences. The differences don't scare us. They stimulate us to understand each other—and ourselves—more deeply. Our world enlarges as we gradually admit each other into our private spaces, including our private religious spaces. My Muslim friends become part of me and I of them. It is such human intermingling that is the real fruit of interreligious dialogue, opening us up to horizons we could never even glimpse if we kept at a "safe" distance from each other.

The present book is no more than an extra tool to help you have the dialogue as well as the fun I've been talking about. May it serve you well!

INDEX

A

Abu Bakr, 21
Acts of the Apostles, book of, 96
afterlife, comparative views on,
  147–152
Ahmad vs. Paraclete, 107–108
Allah
  defined, 8, 14
  generosity of, 18
amr, defined, 48
Arabic language
  comparative difficulty of,
    30–31
  significance for Islam,
    30–32, 124
Arianism, 87
Augustine, Saint, 132

B

Babylonian Exile, 59
Beatitudes, 115–118, 120–121
Bible, versions of, 8
Bin Laden, Osama, 3
bismillah, defined, 156

C

Companions of the Left Hand,
  151–152
Council of Constantinople, 157
Council of Nicaea, 157
creation
  in Genesis account, 43–45
  in Qur'an, 43–44, 45
  as moral example, 47
  of humanity, 51–58
    Genesis account of, 53
    Qur'anic account of, 54
crucifixion
  Gospel accounts of, 93–94
  in the Qur'an, 94

D

Didache, 110
Divine Comedy (Dante), 2

E

Ecumenical Council at
  Chalcedon, 87
Ephesians, Letter to the, 133,
  137

F

Fall, the, 73, 129
First Crusade: A New History, The
  (Asbridge), 137
Five Pillars of Islam. *See* Islam,
  Five Pillars of

G

Genesis, book of, 44–45, 51, 53,
  55, 56–57, 67, 68, 69–71,
  73–74
Gnosticism, 90
God, comparative views on,
  153–158
Gospels, differing accounts in,
  115–116
grace, comparative views on,
  128–129

H

hadith, defined, 123
hajj
  defined, 17
  economic impact of, 19
  customs of, 64
heaven, comparative views on,
  147
hell, comparative views on,
  147–152

Mary
Annunciation to, compar-
ative views on, 75–80, 89,
157
respect for, in Qur'an, 76
virginity of, 83, 103
masjid, defined, 34
Mass, 109
Massignon, Louis, 2
Matthew, Gospel of, 82, 96, 111,
116, 117, 120, 121, 140–141,
148
Mecca, 14, 116, 132
trade in, 15–16
Medina, 14, 132
Modalism, 87
Monophysitism, 87
Muhammad
battles with Quraysh, 22.
See also Quraysh, persecution of Muhammad
childhood of, 15
in Dante's Divine Comedy, 2
hijrah of, 14, 20–22, 132
humanity of, 25
in Mecca, 15–16, 19–20,
22–24
polygamy of, 22
as prophet, 16
as source of Qur'an, 8, 14
Muslim-Christian dialogue, 2,
29, 160–162
Muslims
beliefs about Jesus, 2, 25,
94, 97–101, 144
defined, 17
praying with, 5–6, 113–114
understanding of salvation,
73
views on original sin, 74

N
Nestorianism, 87
Nicene Creed, 87
Nicodemus, 153–154
Nostra Aetate (Declaration on the
Relationship of the Church
to Non-Christian Religions),
1–2, 9

O
"Opening, The," 109
Our Father, 109–110
Muslim views on, 112–113

P
Patriot Act, 160
Paul, Saint, 25, 120, 124, 128,
131, 137
Pentagon. See September 11 terrorist attacks
"People of the Book," Christians
and Jews as, 23–24
Peter, Second Letter of, 116
Philippians, Letter to the, 125,
137
prayer, comparative views on,
109–114

Q
Qur'an
Adam and Eve in, 67–68,
71–72, 73
beauty of, 32–35, 110
Christian understanding of,
30
criticism of Jews, 91, 96, 154
defined, 14, 35
informed knowledge of, 4,
6–7
on Jesus' death and resurrection, 25, 89–96
ambiguity on crucifixion,
95–96